THE
STAND-UP
COMEDY IMPROV
BIBLE

5 in 1

The Ultimate Step-by-Step Guide for Writing,
Performing, and Achieve Success as a
Stand-Up Comic | Easy Techniques to
Conquer the Stage and Slay Hecklers!

Lanny C. Kale

TABLE OF CONTENTS

PART 1: THE FOUNDATIONS OF STAND-UP COMEDY 1

Introduction 2

Chapter 1: Understanding the Art of Stand-Up Comedy 4

The History and Evolution Of Stand-Up Comedy 5
Analyzing Different Comedy Styles.. 8
The Psychology of Humor 10
Exercises: Solo Brainstorming Sessions to Generate Comedy Ideas;
Pair Exercises to Analyze and Critique Different Comedy Styles 15

Chapter 2: Crafting Killer Material 23

Discover Your Authentic Comedy Persona.................................24
Finding Your Unique Comedy Voice 29
Brainstorming Techniques for Comedy Material 33
Crafting Jokes and Punchlines..40
How To Turn Your Problems into Punchlines 45
Structuring Your Set for Maximum Impact.................................54
Create 60 Minutes of New Material..60
Exercises: Solo Joke-Writing Exercises; Pair Exercises to Workshop
and Refine Jokes 64

PART 2: MASTERING PERFORMANCE TECHNIQUES 71

Chapter 3: Mastering Performance Techniques 72

Overcoming Stage Fright.. 73
Developing Confidence and Stage Presence 82
The Art of Timing and Delivery..88
Connecting With Your Audience 93
Exercises: Solo Visualization Exercises for Confident Performance;
Pair Exercises for Practicing Delivery and Timing 98

Chapter 4: Handling Hecklers Like Pro................................... 104

Understanding Heckler Psychology 105
Strategies For Dealing with Hecklers 108
Turning Heckling Situations Into Opportunities 114

Maintaining Control of The Stage... 120
Exercises: Solo Role-Playing Scenarios with Imaginary Hecklers;
Pair Exercises for Practicing Responses to Heckling 124

PART 3: FINE-TUNING YOUR ACT 129

Chapter 5: Fine-Tuning Your Act.. 130

Rehearsal Techniques and Tips 131
Seeking and Incorporating Feedback 138
Refining Your Material for Success.. 145
Push Procrastination and Get Booked....................................... 147
Exercises: Solo Rehearsal Exercises for Perfecting Delivery;
Pair Exercises for Giving and Receiving Feedback on Material 150

PART 4: MARKETING YOURSELF AS A STAND-UP COMIC 157

Chapter 6: Marketing Yourself as a Stand-Up Comic 158

Building Your Brand as A Comedian 159
Utilizing Social Media and Online Platforms 164
Booking Gigs and Networking in The Comedy Industry.................. 167
Exercises: Solo Brainstorming Sessions for Personal Branding; Pair
Exercises for Networking Practice 171

PART 5: MASTERING THE CRAFT OF COMEDY 177

Chapter 7: The Fundamental Elements of Excellent Humor 178

Analyzing What Makes Jokes and Punchlines Work........................ 179
Understanding The Role of Exaggeration and Contrast 183
The Importance of Word Choice And Delivery 186
Exercises: Solo Analysis of Comedic Techniques in Famous Jokes;
Pair Exercises for Practicing Delivery and Timing with Emphasis on Key
Comedic Elements 190

Chapter 8: Steps and Procedures for Creating Material 195

Step-By-Step Guide to Generating Comedy Ideas.............................. 196
Structuring Jokes and Punchlines.. 199
Expressing Material with The Right Technique................................202
Exercises: Solo Brainstorming Sessions Using Specific Comedy-
Generating Techniques; Pair Exercises for Crafting Jokes and
Refining Punchlines 205

Chapter 9: Steps and Procedures for Excellent Performance..................208

Preparing Mentally and Physically for Performances...........................209
Rehearsing With Purpose 212
Developing Stage Presence 214
Exercises: Solo Visualization and Relaxation Exercises for Preparing
for Performances; Pair Exercises for Practicing Stage Presence and
Audience Interaction Techniques...217

Bonus 221

Conclusion 224

PART 1
THE FOUNDATIONS OF STAND-UP COMEDY

INTRODUCTION

Welcome, fellow comedians and aspiring comics! As someone who has spent over a decade working in the comedy industry and helping others hone their craft, I could not be more thrilled to share my knowledge and expertise with you in this comprehensive comedy guide.

When I first started in stand-up comedy, I had no formal training or background in the art of humor. All I had was a love of laughing and a desire to make others laugh in return. However, without proper guidance on how to develop material, overcome stage fright, and handle challenging audiences, those early performances were nothing short of disastrous. I quickly learned just how nuanced the skills of a stand-up comedian truly are. Through years of meticulous study, diligent practice, and hands-on experience on stages both large and small, I evolved as a performer and began to truly understand what it takes to succeed in this field.

Now, as a seasoned veteran with extensive coaching experience under my belt, I have made it my mission to empower new comics with the tools, techniques, and confidence necessary to find their comedic voices and thrive in front of a crowd. Within these pages, you will find all of the hard-won knowledge I have gained distilled into clear, step-by-step guidance. From crafting bulletproof material and conquering stage presence to marketing your brand and navigating the industry, this comprehensive guide covers every aspect of the stand-up process with proven methods and practical exercises.

We will start by delving into the history and psychology of humor so you can appreciate the vast power and nuance of this coveted gift. Understanding what truly makes an audience laugh is the first step towards tapping into those instincts yourself. Next, we will explore various comedy styles and personalities so you can authentically develop your unique comedic flair. Don't worry - through targeted brainstorming sessions and hands-on workshops, you will cultivate an arsenal of hilarious, personal material in no time.

With a solid foundation of expert comedic content in your back pocket, we will then shift our focus to mastering the crucial performance aspects of the trade. Visualization exercises and roleplaying scenarios will help overcome crippling fears, while rigorous rehearsal techniques cultivate confidence, timing, and presence that demands attention on stage. You will also gain invaluable insight into heckler psychology and learn proven strategies for turning hostile interactions into opportunities that engage the whole room.

Our work will then enter the crucial refinement stage. Through self-analysis, peer feedback sessions, and targeted goal setting, you will finesse your act into championship material. We will explore rehearsal methods to prepare for every conceivable performance scenario and push you to start actively booking shows. Once in the driver's seat of your blossoming career, next comes spreading your name with savvy personal branding and aggressive social media marketing prowess.

Finally, as the true grand finale of our intensive coaching program, we will delve into a comprehensive breakdown of the fundamental comedic principles and elements that have stood the test of time. Real-world case studies and insightful workshops will reveal the precise ingredients required for constructing joke architecture that consistently lands. We will also explore how top comics brilliantly apply nuanced performance techniques to breathe vibrant life into their words on stage.

By the end of our journey together, not only will you fully comprehend and appreciate the admirable craft of stand-up comedy in its entirety, but you will also possess a vast arsenal of proven strategies, razor-sharp skills, inspiring motivation, and bulletproof confidence to embark upon a successful career that is all your own. So are you ready to transform yourself from everyday humorists into headline-worthy comedy stars? Let the lessons begin!

CHAPTER 1

UNDERSTANDING THE ART OF STAND-UP COMEDY

Before learning the technical skills of stand-up comedy, it is important to first understand comedy as a sophisticated art form in its own right. The history of stand-up can be traced back to ancient Greek philosophers like Aristotle theorizing about humor, but it was not until the late 19th century that we saw the true genesis of modern stand-up emerge through lone vaudeville entertainers wandering between venues to tell jokes, stories, and songs directly to lively crowds. This tradition continued blossoming throughout the

Jazz Age and was brought to new mainstream prominence post-World War II by pioneering talents like Bob Hope. The counterculture 1960s saw even bolder boundaries being pushed by provocateurs such as Lenny Bruce, who tackled taboo topics. We have since seen the art form evolve across different mediums thanks to groundbreaking comics such as Dave Chappelle and Amy Schumer.

It is also critical to comprehend theories of humor psychology to understand what unconsciously triggers laughter in audiences. Evolutionary psychologists believe laughter originally developed as a way to diffuse tension, strengthen social bonds, and demonstrate higher thinking. This chapter will break down concepts like incongruity resolution, superiority theory, and relief theory to illuminate the profound truths of what makes things comedically funny. With this backdrop in mind, we will also survey the diverse taxonomy of styles within stand-up, such as observational, character-based, edgy, and clean comedy. Case studies of iconic performers like Jerry Seinfeld, Eddie Murphy, and Joan Rivers will provide invaluable insight into prominent personalities and techniques to help discover your own authentic comedic voice.

The History and Evolution Of Stand-Up Comedy

Stand-up comedy is now seen as a prestigious art form, captivating audiences worldwide with insightful social commentary, rapid-fire jokes, and hilarious storytelling. However, the journey of how this craft evolved into the global phenomenon it is today is rarely fully explored. In this comprehensive historical overview, we will trace stand-up comedy's rich lineage from its early roots in ancient Greece to its revolutionary modern progression across different eras. We will showcase iconic figures who fearlessly pushed creative boundaries at each phase and fundamentally changed the landscape of humor forever.

Ancient Origins of Humorous Performance

Many scholars believe that the first comedy performances started in 5th century BCE Athens. During this 'Golden Age of Greek drama,' playwrights like Aristophanes created 'Old Comedy,' making fun of famous politicians and celebrities with funny verses and exaggerated characters on stage for lively audiences. Similarly, the ancient Romans had 'Fescennine' festivals with improvised, bawdy poetry that mocked local dignitaries. Although this was not modern stand-up, these early performances showed humor's power to bring people together, empower them, and provoke important social commentary even in ancient times.

The Vaudeville Era - Formative Foundations of Lone Comic Performance

It was not until the late 19th century that we began to see the true germination of stand-up comedy as we know it today. Emerging alongside the American Vaudeville circuit, traveling 'monologuists' like Weber and Fields pioneered a new solo format of intimate, in-person joke and song-telling aimed directly at eliciting belly laughs from packed theater crowds night after night. Early 'stand-up' icons such as W.C. Fields further elevated one-man acts with snappy patter, sardonic wordplay, and unrivaled comedic timing. By the roaring 1920s Jazz Age, figures like the Marx Brothers were packing concert halls nationwide, cementing comedy as a bankable commercial enterprise.

The Post-War Golden Age and Television's Amplification

After World War II and the ensuing economic boom that stand-up comedy truly became a mainstream cultural juggernaut. Trailblazers like Bob Hope brought one-liners and topical satire to millions through early radio broadcasts and USO tours. Meanwhile, titans like Sid Caesar captivated audiences with landmark live sketch programs on the new medium of television, training a generation of comedians. By the late 1950s, sitcom staples like I Love Lucy and The Honeymooners had America laughing together each week, showcasing comedy's universal power to unite and uplift national spirits.

The Counterculture Revolution and Pushing Creative Boundaries

However, it was the radical social upheaval of the 1960s that transformed comedy from simple escapism into a powerful tool for challenging societal taboos and dissent. Iconoclasts like Lenny Bruce outraged mainstream sensibilities by blending profanity with political commentary in packed auditoriums and smoky underground clubs. Bruce's obscenity trials highlighted humor's ability to drive social change, inspiring '70s anarchists like George Carlin to further push the boundaries of free speech with edgy routines questioning religion and authority. At the same time, pioneering female talents like Joan Rivers shattered glass ceilings and brought stand-up to a whole new mainstream female demographic.

Globalization and New Digital Frontiers

In the late 20th century, comedy became even more popular around the world. International stars like Rowan Atkinson introduced new, funny styles to many people. TV channels like HBO and Comedy Central helped launch the careers of comedians like Eddie Murphy and Jon Stewart. By the year 2000, online platforms like YouTube and Reddit made it possible for new comedians to become famous overnight. Now, in the 2020s, streaming services like Netflix are promoting a wide range of comedy and giving comedians big global stages. As society changes quickly, comedy will keep challenging people's thoughts and breaking traditional ideas with fearless humor.

Pioneering Icons that Revolutionized the Art Form

While this is just a quick look back at stand-up comedy's history, it highlights some of its most important times and the groundbreaking comedians who changed how people think with their innovative skills far ahead of their time. Many other talented comedians also deserve recognition for paving the way. Performers like Weber and Fields pioneered intimate solo acts. W.C. Fields created memorable characters. Bob Hope made comedy popular on a large scale. Lenny Bruce used comedy to protest social issues. Joan Rivers broke barriers. Today, a diverse group of comedians continues to push this art form to new heights. From ancient Greece to modern streaming platforms, stand-up comedy has always evolved, driven by brave performers who use humor to inspire both laughter and social change.

Analyzing Different Comedy Styles

In the diverse world of stand-up comedy, comedians have developed many unique styles and methods to create their jokes and personalities. From observational humor that comments on everyday life to character-driven jokes and clever puns, mastering different styles allows comedians to connect with a wide range of audiences. This comprehensive overview aims to thoroughly analyze the detailed categories of major comedy genres that comedians use, exploring their key features, influential figures, and the impact of each style through careful examination. Understanding these style archetypes can help you refine your own authentic comedic voice and foster creativity in your performances.

Observational Comedy

Observational comedy is a popular modern style where comedians keenly observe everyday life experiences and find humor in the ironic or absurd aspects of mundane events. Pioneered by legendary acts like Jerry Seinfeld and George Carlin, this approach focuses on subtle social observations that feel universally relatable. Topics range from relationships and parenting to traffic or daily annoyances, all exaggerated for comedic effect. The delivery is typically casual with tight pacing, allowing audiences to easily picture themselves in the amusing anecdotes.

Character & Accent-Based Comedy

Character-based comedy involves bringing unique character "types" to life through distinctive accents, mannerisms, or exaggerated personality traits. Icons like Robin Williams excelled at creating hundreds of hilarious caricatures, while comedians like Stewart Lee meticulously craft recurring favorites such as "Pretentious English Bloke." This style demands strong scene-setting abilities and a chameleon-like range for seamless transformations between characters. Maintaining comedic timing and consistent characterizations is challenging but incredibly entertaining when executed well.

Blue Comedy & Raunchy Humor

Blue comedy pushes boundaries with crass language, shock value, or taboo subjects like sex. Pioneered by Lenny Bruce, who mixed politics with obscenity, it challenges conventional standards. Today, comedians like Ricky Gervais and Jimmy Carr excel in wordplay and humor deemed "inappropriate," aiming for audacious laughs. While this style can disturb or offend, careful selection of material is crucial to suit specific audiences.

One-Liners & Pun-Based Comedy

One-liner comedy delights fans with quick, witty jokes packed into a few words. From Mort Sahl to modern Twitter comedians, this style showcases lightning-fast wit and clever wordplay. It requires precise timing and delivery to maximize laughs in minimal time. However, with so few words per joke, precision is essential, and pacing is critical for effective performance.

Storytelling Comedy

Storytelling comedians captivate audiences with long-form narratives that blend humor into vividly described tales from their lives. Rodney Dangerfield and Joan Rivers were masters, using their personalities and flawless memories to spin hilarious stories. This style demands compelling story arcs, impeccable timing, and a strong connection with the audience over longer performances. Master storytellers are able to command any stage with their captivating narratives.

New Character & Improv Comedy

Innovative troupes like The Vacationers, winners of the Canadian Comedy Award, excel in carefully planned improvisation with absurd plots and unpredictable characters. Similarly, the Upright Citizens Brigade theater in the US pioneers long-form comedic scenes and storylines through audience-driven improvisation. These experimental styles inject fresh spontaneity into comedy, ensuring each show is unique and captivating. However, relying on improv skills means shows can vary in consistency.

Politics & Current Events Comedy

This style allows comedians on major platforms to analyze and satirize headline news and socio-political issues. John Oliver's "Last Week Tonight" is renowned for its deep, contextual comedy segments, while podcasts like Chapo Trap House use leftist political comedy to critique cultural extremes. While this approach risks offense or quickly becoming dated, adept execution turns laughter into a tool for insightful commentary. Balancing complexity and audience appeal is challenging but resonant for many viewers.

Understanding these nuanced comedic styles offers insights into diverse veins of humor. With deliberate practice, comedians can fluidly experiment across styles, engaging audiences consistently. Mastery of style fosters the development of a unique comedic voice and offers fresh perspectives, regardless of content. As new hybrid forms and innovative comedians emerge, comedy continues to evolve dynamically.

The Psychology of Humor

What truly explains the mysterious phenomenon we call humor? Why do certain situations, observations or expressions trigger involuntary smiling, chuckling or full-blown belly laughs within us and others? Exploring humor's psychological underpinnings grants deeper comprehension into comedy's ability to transcend logical thought and universally unite humans. This exhaustive analysis dissects leading theories on laughter's evolutionary roots and neurological basis, illuminated by scientific studies on factors impacting our complex humorous reactions. Harnessing such knowledge empowers comedians to more precisely craft content guaranteed to elicit mirth.

Laughter's Evolutionary Origins

Psychologists today widely agree that laughter evolved primarily as a nonverbal social signal rather than solely a physical response to humor. Its origins are hypothesized to date back 65 million years among early primate ancestors, serving as a tool to strengthen social bonds within groups. Laughter acted as an "acoustic marker," reducing tension and showcasing intelligence or status through playful interactions. Similar to chimpanzees using laughter-like panting after conflicts, humans retained this social function throughout cultural evolution. Laughter remains a natural expression of pleasure and solidarity among us.

Neurological Mechanisms Behind Mirth

Modern brain imaging research has provided valuable insights into the specific mechanisms involved in our response to humor. A crucial area is the Ventral Striatum, which plays a key role in processing rewards and pleasure by releasing dopamine, often referred to as "happy hormones." Humor activates this 'pleasure center' more intensely than many other stimuli, second only to activities like sex or eating. Additionally, the Orbitofrontal Cortex detects ambiguities and surprises inherent in humor, further stimulating the reward pathway. Finally, laughter itself is controlled by several brainstem regions linked to the motor control systems of vocalization and facial expressions. Humor effectively influences our neurological pathways related to pleasure and arousal.

Incongruity & Resolution Theories

Incongruity Theory

According to philosophers like Immanuel Kant and Arthur Schopenhauer, Incongruity Theory suggests that humor arises when we encounter ideas, situations, or scenarios that violate our established expectations in a surprising or incongruous way. Comedy often introduces abnormalities or irregularities that contradict standard norms, creating a cognitive dissonance that engages our minds.

Resolution of Incongruity

In this theory, for humor to be maximally effective, the initial incongruity must be resolved in a surprising yet logical manner. Jokes and comedic situations typically offer a resolution that redeems the subverted expectations and rationalizes the preceding absurdity. This resolution returns the situation to a state of normalcy, providing a satisfying catharsis that makes the unpredictability entertaining and memorable.

Patterns in Comedy

Analyzing classic comedy routines and scripts reveals they often follow predictable patterns: introducing unexpected incongruity and then providing a clever resolution that explains the confusion. Audiences familiar with these formulas can anticipate moments of comedic disruption and enjoy the humor of seeing their assumptions violated, only to be cleverly resolved in the end.

Superiority Theories

Superiority and Laughter

According to theories proposed by thinkers like Thomas Hobbes, some theories of humor suggest that laughter arises from recognizing one's own superiority over others or from pointing out their perceived flaws and misfortunes. Laughter can serve as a way to bond socially by collectively acknowledging individuals as inferior. However, humor that involves mean-spirited mockery lacks empathy and can foster contempt instead of fostering unity through humor.

Brain Activation and Humor

Controversially, some scientific evidence suggests that laughing at others may activate areas of the brain associated with social cognition, dominance, and self-representation. This supports theories that humor can satisfy drives related to feelings of superiority. However, successful comedy must ultimately bring audiences together in shared amusement rather than dividing them through ridicule.

Constructive Humility in Comedy

The most effective humor acknowledges life's absurdities without demeaning participants. Instead of targeting individuals, the best comedians often find common ground in universal human follies and hypocrisies that we all experience. By encouraging audiences to laugh together through empathy and egalitarianism, comedy builds social bonds that superiority-based mockery can fracture.

Relief & Release Theories

Release Through Laughter

Pioneered by psychoanalysts like Sigmund Freud, Relief theories propose that laughter acts as a psychological release or safety valve. Humor provides a pathway to safely relieve accumulated mental, emotional, and physical tensions. Laughter emerges as a cathartic expression when triggered by appropriate comedic stimuli.

Physiological Effects of Laughter

Modern scientific research supports this theory by demonstrating laughter's measurable stress-reducing effects on the body. Studies indicate that humor lowers stress hormones such as cortisol and increases the production of endorphins, which are neurotransmitters associated with feelings of well-being. The act of smiling and laughing also relaxes tense muscles and releases built-up arousal. Laughter can thus be seen as a form of psychotherapy with tangible physiological benefits.

Social Benefits of Tension Release

Humor may have evolved as a socially acceptable way to release tension. By alleviating anxieties and inhibitions through laughter, individuals and groups can strengthen bonds through shared amusement. This cathartic release helps diffuse tensions that, if left unresolved, could strain relationships. Regularly experiencing the tension-reducing benefits of humor promotes individual health, happiness, and social cohesion.

Cultural Differences in Humor

In addition to individual factors, the cultural environment heavily impacts what type of humor is found funny.

Sarcasm and Dry Wit

For example, sarcasm tends to be better received in Western cultures that value independence compared to Eastern cultures emphasizing social harmony. The sarcastic and dry wit types of humor more commonly seen in Britain, Canada and other Western nations rely on subverted expectations and implications over overt statements. Conversely, this style does not translate as well in collectively oriented Asian societies.

Taboo Topics

Additionally, taboo topics like politics differ greatly across cultures and political affiliation. What may elicit laughs from a predominantly left-leaning audience may deeply offend those on the right and vice versa. Navigating controversially topical humor necessitates deep understanding audiences' complex norms and biases surrounding off-limit issues.

Group Dynamics

Cultural group dynamics also impact appropriate humor. Cultures emphasizing loyalty to institutions or authorities find disrespecting such figures less humorous. However, humor subverting power structures resonates more strongly with individualistic cultures prioritizing dissent. Reading cultural undercurrents regarding hierarchy informs comedians' contextual audience sensitivities.

Global Perspectives

Understanding these cultural variations is crucial for international comedians to craft material that translates universally. Insight into diverse humorous perspectives cultivates cultural appreciation and more inclusive comedy. Adapting to norms wherever one performs necessitates diligent study of social implications behind any given culture's accepted comedy standards.

Exercises: Solo Brainstorming Sessions to Generate Comedy Ideas; Pair Exercises to Analyze and Critique Different Comedy Styles

Exercise 1: The Observation Odyssey

Duration: 7 days, 30 minutes per day

Objective: Sharpen observational skills and generate comedy material from everyday life.

Step-by-step instructions:

1. Choose 7 diverse locations for the week (e.g., coffee shop, park, public transportation, grocery store, gym, library, shopping mall).
2. Each day, visit one location and find a comfortable spot to observe without drawing attention to yourself.
3. Set a timer for 30 minutes and focus solely on observing your surroundings.
4. In a notebook, jot down at least 30 observations. These can include:
   - People's behaviors and interactions
   - Unusual or quirky details about the environment
   - Overheard conversations or snippets
   - Patterns or routines you notice
   - Your own thoughts or reactions to what you see
5. Don't filter or judge your observations; write down everything, no matter how mundane it may seem.
6. After the 30 minutes, spend an additional 5 minutes reviewing your notes and circling any observations that strike you as potentially humorous or intriguing.
7. At the end of the week, compile all your observations into a single document.
8. Review the compiled list and highlight the top 20 observations that you think have the most comedic potential.
9. For each of these 20 observations, spend 10 minutes free-writing potential comedy angles. Consider:
   - What's unusual or contradictory about this observation?

- How could this be exaggerated for comedic effect?
- Are there any relatable human experiences tied to this observation?
- Can you draw any unexpected connections or comparisons?

10. Select your top 5 developed ideas and expand them into rough 1-minute comedy bits. Focus on:
    - A clear setup that establishes the context
    - A punchline or twist that subverts expectations
    - Additional tags or act-outs that build on the initial joke
11. Practice delivering these bits, paying attention to timing and emphasis.
12. Reflect on the process:
    - Which locations yielded the most fruitful observations?
    - What types of observations translated best into comedy material?
    - How has this exercise changed the way you view your daily surroundings?
13. Moving forward, establish a routine of carrying a small notebook or using a note-taking app on your phone to jot down observations throughout your day. Set a goal to collect at least 10 new observations daily.
14. Weekly, review your collected observations and develop at least one new comedy bit based on them.

By consistently practicing the Observation Odyssey, you'll train your mind to constantly seek out the humorous and absurd in everyday life, building a rich reservoir of material for your comedy writing.

Exercise 2: The Perspective Flip

Duration: 3 hours

Objective: Develop the ability to view situations from multiple angles and generate unique comedic takes.

Step-by-step instructions:

1. Select 5 common situations or experiences (e.g., going on a first date, starting a new job, dealing with a noisy neighbor, trying a new hobby, planning a vacation).

2. For each situation, list 5 different types of people who might experience it. Aim for diversity in age, background, profession, and personality traits.
3. Create a table with the situations as column headers and the person types as row headers.
4. Set a timer for 45 minutes. Working through the table cell by cell, write a brief (2-3 sentence) description of how each person might uniquely experience or react to each situation. Focus on specific details that highlight their perspective.
5. Review your table and identify the 10 most interesting or unexpected perspective/situation combinations.
6. For each of these 10 combinations, spend 10 minutes free-writing a monologue from that person's point of view about the situation. Really inhabit their mindset and voice.
7. Read through your monologues and highlight any lines or ideas that surprise you or make you laugh.
8. Choose your top 3 perspective/situation combinations to develop further.
9. For each chosen combination:
   a. Expand the monologue into a 2-minute comedy bit.
   b. Incorporate specific details that bring the perspective to life.
   c. Find opportunities for act-outs or character voices.
   d. Identify the core humor in the perspective and emphasize it.
10. Practice performing each bit, focusing on fully embodying the character's perspective.
11. Reflect on how seeing situations from different perspectives has generated new comedic ideas:
    • What surprised you about taking on these different viewpoints?
    • Which perspectives were most challenging to inhabit?
    • How can you apply this technique to your regular comedy writing process?
12. Create a "Perspective Bank" document where you list various types of people (by age, profession, personality trait, etc.). Regularly add to this list as you encounter or think of new perspectives.

13. Develop a habit of mentally flipping perspectives when you encounter everyday situations. Ask yourself, "How would X person see this differently?"
14. Once a week, choose a current event or trending topic and apply the perspective flip technique to generate comedy material:
    a. List 5 unique perspectives on the event.
    b. Write a brief comedic take from each perspective.
    c. Develop your favorite into a full bit.

By regularly practicing the Perspective Flip, you'll train yourself to see beyond your own experiences and generate comedy that resonates with a wider audience. This exercise also helps in developing character-based comedy and finding fresh angles on common topics.

Exercise 3: The Metaphor Mixer

Duration: 2 hours

Objective: Enhance your ability to create vivid, unexpected comparisons that add color and originality to your comedy.

Step-by-step instructions:

1. Create three lists of 10 items each:
   - List A: Common emotions or states of being (e.g., anger, confusion, excitement)
   - List B: Everyday objects or activities (e.g., toaster, jogging, doing taxes)
   - List C: Historical events or famous people (e.g., French Revolution, Amelia Earhart)
2. Set a timer for 30 minutes. Randomly select one item from each list and combine them to create unusual metaphors. For example: "Confusion is like a toaster during the French Revolution." Aim to create at least 20 of these random combinations.
3. Review your metaphors and rate them on a scale of 1-5 for humor and vividness.

4. Choose your top 10 metaphors. For each, spend 5 minutes free-writing to expand on the comparison. Ask yourself:
   - What specific aspects of each element make this comparison work?
   - How can you exaggerate or specify the metaphor for greater comedic effect?
   - What absurd scenarios does this metaphor suggest?
5. Select your top 5 expanded metaphors. For each:
   - Craft a setup that naturally leads to the metaphor.
   - Develop 2-3 additional punchlines or tags that build on the initial comparison.
   - Think of a personal anecdote or observation that relates to the metaphor.
6. Combine your developed metaphors into a cohesive 5-minute routine. Focus on:
   - Smooth transitions between metaphors
   - A clear thematic thread linking the comparisons
   - Varying the rhythm and structure of how you present each metaphor
7. Practice delivering your routine, paying special attention to your pacing and emphasis. Metaphors often require a slight pause to let the audience mentally picture the comparison.
8. Reflect on the process:
   - Which types of combinations yielded the most interesting metaphors?
   - How did forcing random connections lead to new comedic ideas?
   - In what ways can vivid metaphors enhance your overall comedy writing?
9. Create a "Metaphor Bank" document. Whenever you encounter an interesting object, event, or concept, add it to the document along with a brief description of its key characteristics.
10. Develop a daily metaphor exercise:
    a. Choose an emotion or experience you had that day.
    b. Set a timer for 5 minutes and write as many metaphors for that experience as possible.
    c. Select your favorite and expand it into a brief comedic bit.

11. Practice incorporating metaphors into casual conversations. Challenge yourself to use at least one vivid comparison in everyday discussions.
12. Analyze the use of metaphors by your favorite comedians:
    - How do they introduce and expand upon their comparisons?
    - What makes their metaphors particularly effective or memorable?

By regularly engaging in the Metaphor Mixer exercise, you'll develop a knack for creating unique, colorful comparisons that can elevate your comedy writing. This skill adds depth to your observational humor and helps create memorable moments in your routines that audiences are likely to remember and share.

Exercise 4: The Premise Perfecter

Duration: 2.5 hours

Objective: Develop the skill of generating strong comedic premises and expanding them into fully-formed bits.

Step-by-step instructions:

1. Warm-up (15 minutes):
   a. Set a timer for 5 minutes and rapidly write down as many random words as you can think of.
   b. Choose 10 words from your list at random.
   c. For each word, spend 1 minute writing a bizarre "what if" scenario involving that word.
2. Premise Generation (30 minutes):
   a. Review your "what if" scenarios and select the 3 most intriguing ones.
   b. For each selected scenario, spend 10 minutes brainstorming potential comedic premises.
      A strong premise should:
      - Present a clear, concise setup
      - Contain an inherent contradiction or absurdity
      - Be relatable or topical
      - Suggest multiple angles for jokes

3. Premise Expansion (45 minutes): Choose your top 2 premises. For each:
    a. Write the premise at the top of a page.
    b. Set a timer for 20 minutes and free-write everything that comes to mind related to the premise. Include:
    - Potential punchlines
    - Personal anecdotes that relate to the premise
    - Absurd consequences of the premise
    - Character voices or act-outs that could enhance the bit
    c. Don't censor yourself; write down every idea, no matter how silly it seems.
4. Bit Construction (40 minutes): For each expanded premise:
    a. Review your free-writing and highlight the strongest ideas.
    b. Organize these ideas into a logical flow, creating a rough outline for your bit.
    c. Craft a strong opening line that clearly establishes your premise.
    d. Develop your main punchlines, ensuring they directly relate to the premise.
    e. Add tags and act-outs to extend the laughs.
    f. Create a strong closing line that callbacks to your premise.
5. Refinement (15 minutes):
    a. Read through both developed bits.
    b. Tighten the language, removing any unnecessary words.
    c. Ensure each line builds towards a laugh.
    d. Identify spots where you can add in quick asides or additional tags.
6. Practice and Reflection (15 minutes):
    a. Stand up and deliver both bits out loud.
    b. Note any areas where the wording feels clunky or the flow is off.
    c. Make quick adjustments based on your performance.
7. Final Analysis: Reflect on the process:
    o Which premises were easier to expand and why?
    o How did the free-writing process contribute to developing your bits?
    o What techniques were most helpful in generating punchlines from your premise?
8. Ongoing Practice: a) Start a "Premise Journal." Each day, write down at least 3 potential comedic premises inspired by your

experiences or observations. b) Weekly, choose your strongest premise and develop it into a full bit using this exercise's process. c) Begin your writing sessions with a 10-minute premise generation warm-up to get your creative juices flowing.

By regularly practicing the Premise Perfecter exercise, you'll strengthen your ability to generate solid comedic foundations and expand them into rich, multi-layered bits. This skill is crucial for developing original material and ensuring your comedy has a strong, focused direction.

Now, let's pair each exercise with an analysis and critique of different comedy styles:

1. The Observation Odyssey pairs with Observational Comedy: Analyze how comedians like Jerry Seinfeld or Jim Gaffigan take everyday observations and transform them into hilarious routines. Critique the balance between relatability and unique perspective in observational humor.
2. The Perspective Flip pairs with Character-Based Comedy: Study the work of comedians like Eddie Murphy or Kate McKinnon who excel at creating distinct personas. Analyze how they use different perspectives to generate humor and critique the depth and consistency of their character work.
3. The Metaphor Mixer pairs with Surrealist or Abstract Comedy: Examine the styles of comedians like Steven Wright or Mitch Hedberg who specialize in unexpected connections and absurd comparisons. Critique the balance between cleverness and accessibility in their material.
4. The Premise Perfecter pairs with Premise-Based Comedy: Analyze comedians like Dave Chappelle or John Mulaney who excel at taking a single premise and exploring it fully. Critique their ability to maintain focus while finding multiple angles on a single idea.

By pairing these exercises with analysis of different comedy styles, you'll deepen your understanding of various approaches to humor and how to apply the skills you're developing to different forms of comedy.

CHAPTER 2
CRAFTING KILLER MATERIAL

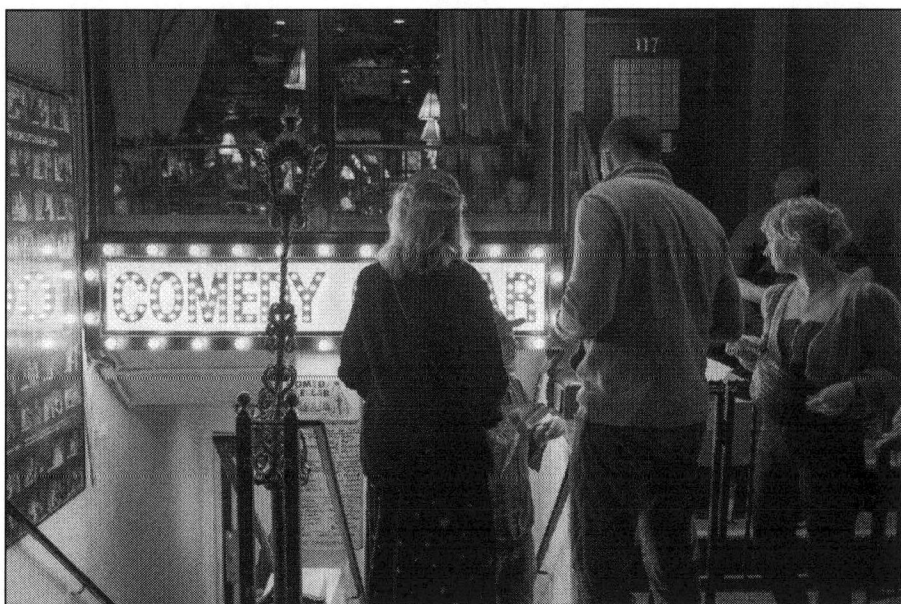

While talent and timing are certainly factors, developing truly great comedy requires dedicated work. This chapter focuses on the essential craft elements for constructing material that kills on stage. Whether aiming to be a stand-up comedian or improve skills for public speaking, learning the fundamentals of effective joke writing, storytelling techniques, and how to refine routines will lead to tighter, polished content that consistently lands.

We'll explore proven methods for sourcing funny ideas from daily life, structuring narratives with impactful comedic beats, sharpening punchlines, and getting honest feedback to refine unfinished drafts.

Mastering the construction aspects of comedy lays the foundation comedians build successful careers upon. The following sections break down actionable strategies for honing your skills as a joke smith and transforming raw musings into killer material that leaves audiences howling every time.

Discover Your Authentic Comedy Persona

In the world of stand-up comedy, authenticity is paramount. Audiences can quickly detect insincerity, and attempts to mimic other comedians or adopt a false persona often fall flat. Your authentic comedy persona should be an extension of your true self, allowing you to tap into your unique experiences, perspectives, and quirks.

Consider the case of Hannah Gadsby, whose groundbreaking special "Nanette" revolutionized the stand-up comedy landscape. Gadsby's authentic approach to discussing her experiences as a queer woman in a conservative society resonated deeply with audiences worldwide. By embracing her true self and sharing her vulnerabilities, Gadsby created a powerful and unforgettable comedic experience.

Self-Reflection and Identifying Your Comedic Strengths

The journey to discovering your authentic comedy persona begins with self-reflection. Ask yourself:

1. What makes you laugh?
2. What unique life experiences have shaped your worldview?
3. What topics are you passionate or knowledgeable about?
4. What aspects of your personality do others find entertaining or endearing?

By answering these questions honestly, you'll start to uncover the building blocks of your comedic persona. For example, Jim Gaffigan's self-deprecating humor and observations about food stem from his Midwestern upbringing and experiences as a father of five. His authentic persona as the relatable "everyman" has made him one of the most successful comedians of his generation.

Embracing Your Quirks and Idiosyncrasies

Often, the aspects of ourselves that we consider flaws or oddities can become our greatest comedic assets. Embracing these quirks can lead to a truly unique and memorable persona. Take Tig Notaro, for instance. Her deadpan delivery and ability to find humor in life's darkest moments, including her battle with cancer, have become hallmarks of her comedic style.

To identify your own quirks that could translate into comedy gold, consider:

- Physical characteristics or mannerisms that people often comment on
- Unusual hobbies or interests
- Recurring patterns in your relationships or daily life
- Peculiar thought processes or observations

Remember, what makes you different is what makes you interesting. Lean into these aspects of yourself to create a persona that stands out from the crowd.

Developing Your Point of View

A crucial element of your comedy persona is your unique point of view. This encompasses your opinions, observations, and the lens through which you see the world. Developing a strong point of view helps you craft material that is distinctly yours and allows audiences to connect with your perspective.

George Carlin's acerbic social commentary and Bill Burr's politically incorrect rants are prime examples of strong comedic points of view. While you don't need to be controversial to have a compelling point of view, you should strive to offer fresh insights on familiar topics or shed light on overlooked aspects of life.

To develop your point of view:

- ✓ Stay informed about current events and popular culture
- ✓ Analyze your reactions to everyday situations
- ✓ Challenge conventional wisdom and explore alternative perspectives
- ✓ Keep a journal of your thoughts and observations

Experimenting with Different Styles and Approaches

Finding your authentic comedy persona often involves trial and error. Don't be afraid to experiment with different styles, topics, and delivery methods. Some comedians, like Bo Burnham, incorporate music and multimedia elements into their acts. Others, like Maria Bamford, use character work and impressions to enhance their material.

To explore different comedic approaches: Attend open mics and try out various styles, Record yourself performing and analyze what works best, Seek feedback from fellow comedians and trusted friends and Study a wide range of comedians to understand different techniques!

Remember that your persona may evolve over time, so remain open to growth and change.

Crafting Your Stage Presence

Your physical presence on stage plays a significant role in your overall comedy persona. This includes your body language, facial expressions, and how you interact with the microphone and stage space. Some comedians, like Jerry Seinfeld, adopt a more reserved and controlled presence, while others, like Robin Williams, were known for their high-energy, physical performances.

To develop your stage presence:

1. Practice in front of a mirror or record yourself performing
2. Experiment with different levels of energy and movement
3. Consider how your physical appearance (clothing, hairstyle, etc.) contributes to your persona
4. Study the body language and stage presence of comedians you admire

Finding Your Comedic Voice

Your comedic voice is the unique way you express yourself through your material and delivery. It encompasses your writing style, word choice, timing, and rhythm. Developing a distinctive voice takes time and practice, but it's essential for creating a memorable and authentic persona.

For example, Mitch Hedberg's surreal one-liners and Steven Wright's deadpan delivery are instantly recognizable comedic voices. To find your own voice:

1. Write extensively and regularly to develop your style
2. Read your material aloud to refine your rhythm and timing
3. Pay attention to your natural speech patterns and incorporate them into your act
4. Experiment with different sentence structures and word choices

Embracing Vulnerability and Honesty

Some of the most powerful and authentic comedy comes from a place of vulnerability and honesty. By sharing personal stories and experiences, you create opportunities for genuine connection with your audience. Comedians like Mike Birbiglia and Hasan Minhaj have built successful careers by crafting deeply personal, narrative-driven stand-up specials.

To incorporate vulnerability into your comedy:

1. Identify experiences or emotions that have had a significant impact on you
2. Practice talking about these topics in a way that feels comfortable and authentic
3. Gradually introduce more personal material into your act
4. Pay attention to audience reactions and adjust accordingly

Consistency and Character Development

As you develop your authentic comedy persona, it's important to maintain consistency across your performances and social media presence. This doesn't mean you can't evolve or explore new territory, but there should be a recognizable thread that ties your work together.

Consider how comedians like Patton Oswalt and John Mulaney have cultivated distinct personas that extend beyond their stand-up acts into their social media, acting roles, and written work. To develop a consistent persona:

1. Identify core traits or themes that define your comedic identity

2. Develop a unique "voice" for your social media presence
3. Look for opportunities to showcase your persona in other mediums (podcasts, writing, acting)
4. Regularly revisit and refine your comedic goals and brand

Navigating Cultural Sensitivity and Inclusivity

In today's diverse and interconnected world, it's crucial to consider how your comedy persona and material might be perceived by different audiences. While pushing boundaries can be an essential part of comedy, it's important to do so thoughtfully and with awareness of potential impacts.

Comedians like Aziz Ansari and Ali Wong have successfully navigated cultural topics by drawing from their personal experiences and offering nuanced perspectives. To create an authentic persona that remains sensitive to cultural issues:

1. Educate yourself on diverse perspectives and experiences
2. Be willing to listen and learn from feedback
3. Consider the intent and impact of your material
4. Use your platform responsibly to address important issues when appropriate

Embracing Failure and Learning from Mistakes

Developing your authentic comedy persona is an ongoing process that involves many failures and missteps along the way. Embracing these moments as learning opportunities is crucial for growth and refinement of your comedic identity.

Even highly successful comedians like Dave Chappelle and Chris Rock continue to work on new material at small clubs, understanding that failure is an integral part of the creative process. To make the most of your failures:

1. Keep a record of what works and what doesn't in your performances
2. Analyze why certain jokes or approaches didn't land with the audience
3. Be willing to abandon or rework material that consistently underperforms

4. Seek constructive feedback from peers and mentors in the comedy community

Finding Your Unique Comedy Voice

Your comedy voice is the authentic expression of your comedic point of view. It encompasses your subject matter, delivery style, persona on stage, and the unique way you see the world. Think of it as your comedic fingerprint - no two are exactly alike. Legendary comedians like Richard Pryor, Joan Rivers, and Dave Chappelle are instantly recognizable because they've developed strong, unique voices.

The cornerstone of finding your comedy voice is authenticity. Audiences can sense when a performer is genuine, and they respond to honesty. Comic Tig Notaro's career-defining moment came when she performed a set about her cancer diagnosis, turning a deeply personal struggle into powerful, authentic comedy. By embracing vulnerability and truth, she connected with audiences on a profound level.

Embracing Your Background and Experiences

Your unique life experiences are a goldmine for comedic material. Ali Wong's comedy specials draw heavily from her experiences as an Asian-American woman, wife, and mother. By leaning into her background, she's created a voice that's distinctly her own. Similarly, Hannah Gadsby's groundbreaking special "Nanette" used her experiences as a queer woman from Tasmania to challenge the very structure of stand-up comedy.

Identifying Your Comedic Strengths

Are you naturally witty with quick comebacks? Perhaps you excel at storytelling or have a knack for physical comedy. Identifying your strengths can help shape your voice. Jim Gaffigan, for instance, is known for his observational humor and his "inner voice" technique, where he comments on his own jokes in a high-pitched whisper. This unique approach has become a signature part of his comedy voice.

Experimenting with Different Styles

Finding your voice often involves trying on different comedic styles to see what fits. You might explore:

1. Observational comedy (e.g., Jerry Seinfeld)
2. Character-based comedy (e.g., Sacha Baron Cohen)
3. Deadpan delivery (e.g., Steven Wright)
4. Surrealist humor (e.g., Mitch Hedberg)
5. Political satire (e.g., John Oliver)

Don't be afraid to mix and match elements from different styles. Bo Burnham, for example, combines musical comedy with meta-commentary and absurdism to create his unique voice.

Developing Your Point of View

Your comedic point of view is the lens through which you see the world. It's shaped by your beliefs, experiences, and observations. George Carlin's acerbic commentary on American culture and politics was a direct result of his skeptical, anti-establishment point of view. To develop your own:

1. Stay informed about current events and popular culture
2. Reflect on your personal experiences and how they've shaped your worldview
3. Question societal norms and look for absurdities in everyday life
4. Keep a journal of your thoughts and observations

Writing Consistently

Finding your voice requires consistent practice. Set aside time each day to write, even if it's just for 15 minutes. Not everything you write will be gold, but the act of writing regularly will help you discover patterns in your thinking and humor.

Patton Oswalt famously challenged himself to write five new pages of material every day for a year. This discipline not only improved his writing skills but also helped him refine his voice and generate an abundance of material.

Embracing Failure and Learning from It

Failure is an inevitable part of the process. Even seasoned comedians bomb occasionally. The key is to learn from these experiences. After a notorious failed performance at a corporate event, Pete Davidson used the experience as material for his next special, turning a potentially career-damaging moment into relatable, self-deprecating comedy.

While your comedy voice is personal, developing it doesn't have to be a solitary journey. Seek feedback from fellow comedians, audience members, and even friends and family. Many comedians start by performing at open mics, where they can test material and get immediate audience reactions.

Collaborating with other comedians can also help you refine your voice. The podcast boom has provided a platform for comedians to interact and riff off each other. Shows like "Comedy Bang! Bang!" have become incubators for comedic voices, allowing performers to experiment in a low-pressure environment.

Studying the Greats (Without Imitating Them)

Analyzing successful comedians can provide insights into what makes a strong comedic voice. Study a diverse range of comedians to understand how they've developed their unique styles. However, be cautious about imitating them too closely. The goal is to learn from their techniques and apply those lessons to your own authentic voice.

For example, John Mulaney's storytelling style is influenced by the pacing and structure of classic sitcoms, but he applies this influence to his own experiences and observations, creating something entirely his own.

Adapting to Different Mediums

In today's digital age, comedians have more platforms than ever to showcase their voice. Your comedic voice should be adaptable to different mediums while remaining true to your core identity. Consider how your voice might translate to:

1. Stand-up specials
2. Podcasts
3. Social media (e.g., Twitter, TikTok)

4. Web series
5. Traditional media (TV shows, movies)

Comedians like Phoebe Waller-Bridge have successfully adapted their voice across multiple mediums, from stage shows to TV series like "Fleabag."

Evolving Your Voice Over Time

Your comedic voice isn't static; it should evolve as you grow and change. Many successful comedians have distinct phases in their careers. Eddie Murphy's raw, boundary-pushing comedy of the 1980s evolved into a more family-friendly style in later years. Dave Chappelle's recent specials reflect a more contemplative, provocative voice compared to his earlier work.

Don't be afraid to let your voice change as you gain new experiences and perspectives. Authenticity means staying true to who you are in the present, not who you were when you started.

As your voice develops and gains attention, you'll inevitably face criticism. Some may not connect with your style or may find your material offensive. While it's important to be open to constructive feedback, it's equally crucial to stay true to your authentic voice.

Sarah Silverman's career is a testament to navigating this balance. Known for her edgy, often controversial humor, she's faced significant backlash at times. However, she's managed to evolve her voice while maintaining her core identity, addressing criticisms thoughtfully without abandoning her comedic essence.

The Role of Vulnerability in Developing Your Voice

Embracing vulnerability can be a powerful tool in developing a unique and relatable comedy voice. By sharing personal stories and insecurities, you create opportunities for genuine connection with your audience. Mike Birbiglia's shows often center around deeply personal, sometimes uncomfortable experiences, turning potential embarrassments into comedic gold.

Finding your comedy voice is not an overnight process. It requires consistent effort, patience, and a willingness to evolve. Even established comedians continue to refine their voices throughout their careers. Gary Gulman, despite being in the industry for decades, experienced a career resurgence with his special "The Great Depresh," where he opened up about his struggles with depression, adding new depth to his comedic voice.

Brainstorming Techniques for Comedy Material

For any comedian or humor writer, having a constant stream of fresh ideas is essential for crafting new, engaging routines and content. However, coming up with comedy concepts on demand can often feel like a real struggle. This is where effective brainstorming techniques become invaluable. In this section, we will explore a variety of proven methods and activities for stimulating comedy idea generation. From journaling daily observations to holding writing sprints with creative constraints, readers will learn tried and tested processes to fuel their humor pipelines. With consistent brainstorming practice, comedians can develop a bounty of raw materials to draw from for developing tighter, audience-tested routines.

Journaling Daily Observations

One of the most fruitful brainstorming activities is simply chronicling observations of amusing interactions, overheard conversations, bizarre behaviors or ironic situations witnessed over the course of a normal day.

Note-Taking Practice

Carry a journal or notes app always to quickly capture amusing quotes, interactions, non sequiturs or quirky occurrences daily. Note-taking trains humor perception. Jot down musings, thoughts or ideas whenever inspiration strikes to review later. Note subtle details and your reactions to fuel potential bits.

Detailed Observational Skills

Train attentiveness to nuanced comedy fodder developing powers of observation and description through thorough documentation. Hone skills of perception by re-readings past notes to uncover more amusement. Over time, notes become a treasure trove of material.

Quote Bank Harvest

Overheard phrases, malapropisms or witticisms offer ripe joke-spinning potential when recorded verbatim in moment. Record quotes exactly as said for authenticity in future comedy. Note context and delivery for potential character material.

Pattern Recognition

Analyze for recurring irony or sub-stories in human behavior becoming rich vein for humor once themes emerge over time. Identify trends across interactions, locations or types of people. Connect related notes into longer narrative observations.

Lighthearted Lens

Seek out funny everywhere through a keen, yet harmless, comedic perspective catching simple pleasures and ironies in mundanity. Notice humor without judgment and with an emphasis on inherent absurdities. Note your perspective shifts which find new amusement.

Humor in Unlikely Places

Notice the absurd or amusing lurking in any situation however unlikely, like standing in long lines or commuting, through your comedy filter. Note sensory details, emotions and ironic contradictions many might overlook.

Harvesting from Experiences

Mining one's own life for comedic moments, mishaps, relationships or adventures offers a seemingly limitless resource.

Revisit Memories Frequently

Make time regularly to reminisce past years through journaling, photos or discussions. Fresh perspectives inspire new humor. Jot down any amusing anecdotes, events or personality quirks you recall.

Analyze Formative Years

Childhood, school days and youth provide treasure troves of mortifying moments, silly situations and social observations. Note cringeworthy moments as well as triumphs.

Mine Relationships

Interpersonal quirks, inside jokes and shared histories offer material, especially with family/friends open to gentle spoofing. Get permission. Ask others to share their memories of you as well.

Highlight Pivotal Events

Triumphs, mishaps, rites of passage humorously encapsulate inherent flaws/virtues comedians recognize in themselves. Retell with humor and self-awareness.

Record Vacation/Hobby Tales

Travelogues, conventions or creative pursuits yield character types and opportunities for mockery involving odd scenarios. Jot down eccentric encounters.

Draw Out Conversation

Ask others to revisit your history together, prompting details which may prove comedic fodder if handled respectfully. Compare perspectives for fresh takes.

Autobiographical experiences offer seemingly inexhaustible material by revisiting colorfully from a wiser, more reflective place with time's advantages. Note lessons learned as well as laughs.

Setting Writing Sprints

A writing sprint involves setting a short time limit (such as 10-15 minutes) to rapidly generate as many ideas, jokes or concepts as possible without self-editing. These constrained creative sessions force the comedian into a flow state where inhibitions fall away and unconventional connections spark novel humor. Try sprints with specific targets like "50 one-liner ideas about dating" to hyper-focus creativity. Set a timer and write non-stop until time expires to push your limits. Varied daily targets keep sprints feeling fresh. Review sprint notes regularly for material to develop further.

Brainstorming with Constraints

Placing unique constraints during an ideation session challenges the comedian's mind to think differently. *For example*, conceiving of jokes using only three words, crafting skits centered around a single prop, or hashing out monologues where every sentence starts with "And then..." stimulates new synaptic pathways towards comedy. Working within boundaries stimulates fresh perspectives. Be wild and experimental with constraints, and don't censor weird ideas. Over time, you'll extend your comedic range. Get even more absurd with constraints to unlock your most bizarre humor.

Playing "What If" Games

Imagining "what if" absurd scenarios can unlock comedic premises, for instance: "What if sneezes could be aimed like a gun?", "What if you couldn't tell lies on Mondays?" or "What if pets could talk?". Sillier the hypothetical, weirder the humor concepts birthed. No parameters remain in these unhinged sessions fueling wacky gags. Play for as long as silly scenarios keep flowing. Get weirder and more fantastical with hypotheses. Note all ideas for reviewing later as premises. Let your oddest mind run free without boundaries. Riff on other people's "what ifs" to build upon the absurdity. Combine unrelated hypotheticals for cross-pollinated hilarity.

Riffing off Prompts

Comedians can brainstorm by riffing off random prompt words, hashtags, audience suggestions, current trends/fads, photos or headlines. The stimulus may spark original jokes, characters, skit ideas or premises by making unexpected comedic connections. Prompts introduce a fun constraint awakening new realms of association. Keep a running list of prompts to revisit for additional material. Encourage others to provide prompts as it sparks their own amusement too. Bounce new ideas off of friends for feedback and collaboration.

Stream of Consciousness Freewriting

Sitting down with a page and pen and simply writing whatever nonsensical thoughts arise can unearth absurd snippets of brilliance buried within random musings. With no editing or pausing, uncensored associations naturally assemble into surreal scenarios ripe for humor mining. Freewriting spawns strange seeds for cultivation. Let the train of thought go in any direction without hesitation or overthinking. Circumvent logic and embrace the nonsensical. Record stream-of-consciousness in daily life too through notes. Revisit freewriting sessions to find recurring comedic concepts worth expanding.

Mind mapping Concept Webs

Creating a visual mind map allows the comedian to branch out ideas in a non-linear way, mapping interconnecting concepts, jokes and premises radiating from central images or words. Webbing stimulates crossover thinking seeing potential for spin-offs stemming from initial branches. Maps generate new routes for comedy voyages. Record all mind maps and revisit for further extrapolations. Color code idea categories to visualize relationships at a glance. Scan maps for recurring themes suitable as full routines. Share maps online to crowdsource additional branches from other creatives. Update maps regularly as new jokes hit. Maps evolve endlessly. Display maps prominently for constant inspiration replay.

Brain Dumping Lists

Similar to sprint sessions, create categorized lists for joke ideas, character types, situational premises, props or absurd concepts. By grouping and building on entries, new connections form between discrete items compounding into more robust routines. Lists breed humor multiplication. Note any items sparking tangents for follow-up pages of associated hunches. Add subcategories to organize. List prompts expansion by periodically challenging oneself to augment sections. Combine seemingly unrelated lists for unexpected guffaws. Review lists across devices and contexts to discover missed links. Lists prove living documents constantly growing more robust.

Reverse Engineering Mainstream Comedy

Studying structures, pacing and creativity of existing successful acts provides invaluable lessons for innovation. Examining formatting, writing techniques or observational styles and mentally "reverse engineering" the humor inspires fresh takes reflecting on techniques that work universally. Learning from leaders primes one's own pipelines. Analyze elements sparking most durable laughs for your toolbox. Pay attention to details which uniquely brand the given artist. Consider lessons in marketing, social strategies and work ethic too. Leaders innovate constantly - remain students and keep learning from the best. Refine by always challenging default assumptions.

Mining from Interests and Passions

Incorporating deep-dive explorations of favorite topics, quirky hobbies, obscure knowledge bases and bizarre fascinations into ideation cultivates material emanating from genuine enthusiasm and curiosity. Coming at interests from an unexpected angle often sparks new jokes or premises bridging subcultures with mainstream relatability. Passion projects energize ideas. Maintain lifelong learning curiosity beyond fleeting trends. Delve into any niche sparking zeal. Note unexpected parallels between hobbies or obsession's. View interests from an outsider's bemused perspective. Combine fascinations in unorthodox mash-ups inspiring fresh premises. Authentic fervor fuels sustainable, soulful comedy.

Harvesting Feedback and Workshopping

Regularly debriefing and fine-tuning concepts through exploratory sessions with writing partners, test audiences or improv games fosters comedy collaboration accelerating ideation. Outside perspectives introduce novel angles igniting further inspiration through fresh combinations and adaptations explored communally. Feedback breeds exponential brainstorming benefits. Apply critique constructively without taking failures personally to continue improving. Seeing multiple angles keeps material versatile.

Incubating Concepts

The creative incubator allows ideas to marinate and hatch by revisiting notes from past sessions or incomplete outlines periodically. Over time, jokes may unexpectedly crystalize or premises organically evolve into more robust, multi-layered formats. Taking breaks enables the subconscious to percolate connections between scattered concepts. Incubation nurtures invisible humor growth. Revisit older drafts with fresh eyes after time away to catch innovations missed earlier. Shift contexts like environments or mindsets to incubate differently. Review regularly for ripening material.

Extracting Gold from Critiques

Though painful initially, critical feedback refines material when mined for gems. Analyze weak spots and strengths noted to selectively strengthen development. Separate critique of specific jokes from personal assessment. External views offer unique angles - integrate the most constructive. Tough feedback expedites evolution when embraced properly.

Evolving Through Iteration

Concepts gain depth and appeal exponentially through repeatedly workshopping variations. Continuous tweaking fosters intimate understanding letting comedians remix elements endlessly. Iteration cultivates ownership and hones in on each concept's comedic core. Commit to ongoing development over spontaneous abandonment for sustainable progress.

Observing Spontaneous Collaborations

Loose jam sessions generate unexpected comedy chemistry worth studying. Note patterns of what provokes others' amusement. Pay attention to group dynamics sparking uncensored giggles. These unplanned insights on human comedy inspire careful application to pre-written material.

Consistently practicing varied brainstorming techniques enables comedians to stockpile a vast arsenal of potential comedy material. With committed ideation over time, raw jewels emerge ready for crafting into compelling, crowd-tested routines fueling any humor career. Creativity thrives through dedicated idea generation.

Crafting Jokes and Punchlines

The art of crafting jokes and punchlines is at the heart of comedy writing. Whether you're working on stand-up material, sketch comedy, or sitcom scripts, understanding the mechanics of joke construction can elevate your comedy to new heights. Let's delve into the techniques, structures, and principles that go into creating effective jokes and memorable punchlines.

The Anatomy of a Joke

At its core, a joke typically consists of two main parts:

1. The Setup: This is the part that establishes the premise and creates expectations.
2. The Punchline: This is the twist that subverts those expectations, creating surprise and (hopefully) laughter.

Understanding this basic structure is crucial, but the real art lies in how you manipulate and play with it.

The Element of Surprise

Surprise is the lifeblood of comedy. Your audience should never see the punchline coming, yet it should feel inevitable in retrospect. Comedian Emo Philips demonstrates this beautifully in his joke:

Setup: "I was walking down the street the other day when I saw my friend George. I thought to myself, 'That's odd. I thought George was...'"

Punchline: "...taller.'"

The audience expects the setup to end with "dead" or something similarly dramatic, making the mundane punchline surprisingly funny.

Misdirection and the Rule of Three

One effective technique for creating surprise is misdirection, often employed using the "rule of three." This involves establishing a pattern with two similar items and then breaking it with a third, unexpected item. For example:

"I have three kids: Sally, who's 10, Tommy, who's 8, and a headache, which is constant."

The first two items set up an expectation, which the third item humorously subverts.

Timing and Delivery

While timing is often associated with performance, it's crucial in writing as well. The placement of your punchline can make or break a joke. Generally, you want the funniest word or phrase to come at the very end of your sentence. Consider this joke by Mitch Hedberg:

"I haven't slept for ten days, because that would be too long."

The punchline, "too long," comes at the very end, maximizing its impact.

Callbacks and Running Gags

Callbacks involve referencing an earlier joke later in your set or script. They create a sense of continuity and reward attentive audience members. Running gags are similar but involve repeating and evolving a joke throughout a performance or series.

For example, in the TV show "Arrested Development," the phrase "I've made a huge mistake" becomes a running gag, gaining humor through repetition and variation.

Specificity in Language

Using specific, vivid language can enhance the humor of your jokes. Compare these two versions of the same joke:

1. Version 1: "I saw a weird animal the other day."
2. Version 2: "I saw a three-legged albino squirrel wearing a tiny sombrero the other day."

The second version paints a much funnier picture due to its specificity.

The Power of Contrast

Contrasting elements can create humor. This could be a contrast in tone, scale, or perspective. Steven Wright's deadpan delivery contrasts with the absurdity of his jokes:

"I went to a restaurant that serves 'breakfast at any time.' So I ordered French Toast during the Renaissance."

The contrast between the mundane (ordering breakfast) and the absurd (time travel) creates the humor.

Subverting Clichés

Taking a well-known phrase or cliché and twisting it can yield great comedic results. Comedian Stewart Francis does this brilliantly:

"You know what I hate about people who criticize you? They're always right."

The expected ending ("They're never right") is subverted, creating surprise.

The "Double Reverse"

This advanced technique involves setting up an expectation, subverting it, then subverting it again. Comedian Anthony Jeselnik is a master of this:

"My girlfriend loves to eat chocolate. She's always eating chocolate, and she likes to joke she's got a chocolate addiction. 'Get me away from those Hersheys!' She loves her chocolate. She kept eating it, and I finally said, 'You really need to stop.' And she said, 'Why?' I said, 'Because you're getting fat.' She said, 'You're rude.' I said, 'No, I'm not. I'm just being honest. And as a friend, I have to tell you that you've gotten fat.' She said, 'That's mean.' I said, 'I know. That's why I didn't want to tell you.'"

The joke sets up an expectation (criticizing chocolate addiction), subverts it (criticizing weight), then subverts it again (admitting to meanness).

The Art of Self-Deprecation

Self-deprecating humor can be very effective when done right. It makes you relatable and disarms the audience. Comedian Rodney Dangerfield built his entire persona around self-deprecation:

"I told my wife the truth. I told her I was seeing a psychiatrist. Then she told me the truth: that she was seeing a psychiatrist, two plumbers, and a bartender."

Crafting Visual Punchlines

Not all punchlines need to be verbal. In visual mediums like sketch comedy or sitcoms, the punchline can be a sight gag. The key is to set up the expectation verbally and then subvert it visually.

For instance, in the show "Brooklyn Nine-Nine," there's a scene where Captain Holt describes a plain beige hat as a "real conversation starter." The visual of the utterly boring hat contrasts humorously with his statement.

The Importance of Economy

In joke writing, brevity is indeed the soul of wit. Every word should serve a purpose, either in setting up the joke or delivering the punchline. Unnecessary words can dilute the impact of your joke.

Consider this one-liner by Jimmy Carr:

"Venison's deer, isn't it?"

The joke relies on the double meaning of "dear/deer" and is perfectly economical.

Crafting Punchlines for Different Comedy Styles

Different styles of comedy require different approaches to punchlines:

1. Observational Comedy: The punchline often highlights the absurdity in everyday situations. Jerry Seinfeld's "What's the deal with..." jokes fall into this category.
2. Anecdotal Comedy: The punchline is the climax of a personal story, often exaggerated for effect. Mike Birbiglia's long-form stories build to carefully crafted punchlines.
3. One-liners: The setup and punchline are condensed into a single sentence. Milton Jones excels at these: "I was watching the London Marathon and saw one runner dressed as a chicken and another runner dressed as an egg. I thought: 'This could be interesting.'"

4. Character Comedy: The punchline often comes from the character's unique perspective or quirks. Think of Borat's misunderstandings of American culture.

Testing and Refining

Joke writing is an iterative process. What seems hilarious on paper might fall flat in front of an audience. Comedy clubs' open mic nights are valuable for testing new material. Pay attention to where people laugh, where they don't, and adjust accordingly.

Sometimes, minor tweaks in wording or delivery can significantly improve a joke. Don't be afraid to workshop your material extensively.

Avoiding Offensive Humor

While pushing boundaries can be part of comedy, it's important to consider the impact of your jokes. Punching down (mocking those with less power) is generally frowned upon in modern comedy. Instead, aim to punch up or, better yet, find ways to make your point without targeting specific groups.

Hannah Gadsby's groundbreaking special "Nanette" challenges the very structure of self-deprecating humor from a marginalized perspective, demonstrating how comedy can evolve and tackle serious issues.

The Role of Truth in Comedy

Many great comedians argue that the best comedy comes from truth. This doesn't mean your jokes need to be factually accurate, but they should resonate with a kernel of emotional or experiential truth.

George Carlin's biting social commentary was funny precisely because it highlighted uncomfortable truths about society. Similarly, Dave Chappelle's ability to tackle race relations comes from his lived experiences and observations.

How To Turn Your Problems into Punchlines

Transforming personal struggles into comedy gold is a time-honored tradition in stand-up. From Richard Pryor's raw confessionals to Hannah Gadsby's groundbreaking "Nanette," comedians have long mined their hardships for laughs. This approach not only creates relatable material but can also be therapeutic for both the performer and the audience. Let's explore how you can alchemize your problems into punchlines.

Embrace Vulnerability

Embracing vulnerability in comedy means being open and honest about personal struggles, insecurities, or challenges. It involves sharing these experiences authentically with an audience, which can create a deep connection and resonance.

Importance of Vulnerability

- **Connection:** When comedians share vulnerable aspects of their lives, it allows the audience to relate on a human level. This connection fosters empathy and understanding.
- **Authenticity:** Genuine vulnerability adds depth and authenticity to comedic material. It shows courage and allows comedians to explore themes that resonate universally.
- **Humor as Coping Mechanism:** By transforming personal struggles into humor, comedians not only entertain but also provide a new perspective on difficult topics, often making them easier to confront.

Maria Bamford exemplifies embracing vulnerability in comedy through her openness about mental health issues. In her special "The Special Special Special," performed in a personal setting (her parents' living room), she candidly discusses her experiences with bipolar disorder and anxiety. This intimate setting, with only her parents as the audience, enhances the vulnerability of her performance. By sharing her struggles with mental health, Bamford turns potentially sensitive topics into comedic gold, eliciting both laughter and reflection from her audience.

Find the Universal in the Personal

Finding the universal in personal experiences is crucial in comedy to ensure that your material resonates with a wide audience. While personal experiences may vary, the underlying emotions and themes are often shared among people. Identifying these universal themes allows comedians to create jokes that connect deeply with their audience. When an audience sees their own experiences reflected in comedic material, it enhances the connection and makes the humor more impactful. Finding the universal in the personal expands the potential audience for comedic material, as it speaks to common human experiences and emotions.

Ali Wong's "Baby Cobra" special is a notable example of finding universality in personal experiences. Despite the specific focus on pregnancy and motherhood, Wong's jokes about body changes, relationship dynamics, and anxieties resonated widely beyond just expectant mothers. By tapping into these universal themes, Wong made her comedy accessible and relatable to a broad audience.

Use Exaggeration and Absurdity

Exaggeration and absurdity are powerful comedic tools that involve amplifying ordinary problems or situations to extreme and often ridiculous levels. This technique not only enhances humor but also paradoxically makes the issues more relatable by highlighting their absurdity.

Importance in Comedy

- **Enhanced Humor:** Exaggeration magnifies the trivial or mundane aspects of problems, turning them into laugh-out-loud scenarios.
- **Emotional Release:** By exploring absurdity, comedians can offer a cathartic release for both themselves and their audience, making challenging topics easier to digest.
- **Universal Appeal:** Absurdity often exposes the underlying ridiculousness in everyday situations, resonating with a broad audience who can recognize similar experiences in their own lives.

John Mulaney frequently uses exaggeration and absurdity in his comedy, particularly when discussing anxiety and awkward situations. For instance, in his routine about anxiety, he exaggerates his nervousness about a routine medical exam, turning a mundane event into a comedic spectacle that resonates with many.

Employ Self-Deprecation (Carefully)

Self-deprecating humor involves making jokes at one's own expense, highlighting personal flaws, quirks, or embarrassing situations. When used effectively, it can create a humorous connection with the audience and turn personal challenges into comedic material.

Balancing Act

- **Humor vs. Negativity:** The key is to strike a balance between humorously acknowledging personal shortcomings and avoiding overly negative or pity-seeking remarks.
- **Audience Connection:** Self-deprecating humor can foster a sense of authenticity and vulnerability, making the comedian more relatable to the audience.
- **Empowerment through Humor:** By laughing at oneself, comedians can reclaim potentially embarrassing or challenging situations, empowering themselves and entertaining others in the process.

Conan O'Brien frequently employs self-deprecating humor in his comedy, particularly regarding his physical appearance and social awkwardness. In his "Conan Without Borders" travel specials, he humorously acknowledges his pale complexion and tall, lanky stature, often joking about feeling out of place in various cultural settings. This self-awareness and willingness to laugh at himself not only endears him to the audience but also turns his experiences into comedic gold.

Use Contrast and Misdirection

Contrast and misdirection are comedic techniques that involve juxtaposing unexpected elements or leading the audience towards one expectation before delivering a surprising twist or punchline. These techniques play with expectations and create humor through surprise and irony.

Importance in Comedy

- **Surprise Factor:** By contrasting serious or unexpected topics with lighthearted or mundane elements, comedians can catch audiences off guard, eliciting laughter from the unexpectedness of the contrast.
- **Subverting Expectations:** Misdirection involves setting up an expectation through storytelling or setup, only to deliver a punchline or conclusion that diverges sharply from what the audience anticipates.
- **Emotional Impact:** Effective use of contrast and misdirection can evoke a range of emotions from laughter to introspection, making the humor more impactful and memorable.

Tig Notaro's set about her cancer diagnosis is a poignant example of using contrast and misdirection in comedy. She begins her routine with the starkly honest line, "Hello, I have cancer. How are you?" This immediate juxtaposition of a casual greeting with the gravity of her diagnosis creates an uncomfortable but surprisingly humorous moment. The audience's initial shock gives way to laughter, setting the tone for Notaro's groundbreaking and deeply personal performance.

Contrast and Misdirection Jokes

- **Joke 1:** "My fear of public speaking is so bad, I once volunteered to give a speech and ended up reading the entire phonebook just to avoid saying anything meaningful."
- **Joke 2:** "I tried conquering my fear of public speaking by imagining the audience naked. Turns out, they were actually the world's top fashion models. Now I have a fear of public speaking and a complex about my wardrobe."
- **Joke 3:** "My attempts at public speaking are like trying to perform Shakespeare in a room full of toddlers—lots of confusion, zero applause, and someone inevitably cries."

Find the Irony

Irony in comedy involves highlighting situations where there is a contrast between expectations and reality, often resulting in humor due to the unexpected or paradoxical nature of the outcome.

Importance in Comedy

- **Unexpected Twists:** Irony adds depth to comedic narratives by presenting situations where the outcome is contrary to what is expected or intended.
- **Humor in Contrast:** By pointing out irony, comedians can draw attention to absurdities or contradictions in everyday life, inviting audiences to laugh at the quirks of human experience.
- **Reflection and Insight:** Irony can also provoke thought and introspection, making audiences reconsider common assumptions or perceptions through a comedic lens.

Marc Maron's comedy often revolves around ironic situations in his life, such as his podcast initially being a last-ditch effort to salvage his career but eventually becoming a major success. This success, ironically, introduces new anxieties and challenges, illustrating how solving one problem can sometimes lead to unexpected consequences.

Identifying Ironical Aspects

- **Ironic Aspect 1:** "I strive for work-life balance so much that my pursuit of relaxation has become a stressful endeavor. It's like jogging to unwind and ending up in a marathon."
- **Ironic Aspect 2:** "I finally mastered work-life balance, only to realize that all my friends and family are now on different schedules, and I have no time left to actually see them."
- **Ironic Aspect 3:** "Achieving work-life balance feels like trying to balance on a seesaw with an elephant and a mouse—either I'm overwhelmed by work or feeling guilty for not doing enough."

Use Analogies and Metaphors

Analogies and metaphors in comedy involve comparing your problems or situations to unrelated concepts, creating surprising and humorous perspectives that highlight the absurdity or intensity of the situation.

Importance in Comedy

- **Fresh Perspectives:** Analogies and metaphors offer new ways to view familiar problems, injecting creativity and humor into storytelling.
- **Visual Imagery:** Vivid comparisons paint a humorous picture in the audience's mind, enhancing the comedic impact of the joke.
- **Unexpected Connections:** Connecting unrelated concepts can surprise audiences, making them laugh at the unexpected but fitting similarities.

Pete Holmes uses analogies effectively in his comedy, such as comparing his divorce to "an alien bursting out of my chest, but in slow motion." This analogy creates a vivid and humorous image of emotional pain, turning a serious topic into something unexpectedly comical.

Unusual Analogies

- **Analogy 1:** "Writer's block feels like trying to swim in a pool full of Jell-O—every stroke takes immense effort, and you're not sure if you're moving forward or just sinking deeper."
- **Analogy 2:** "Facing writer's block is like trying to navigate through a maze where all the walls are made of my own unfinished thoughts—constantly hitting dead ends and retracing my steps."
- **Analogy 3:** "Writer's block is like being trapped in a library full of books written in a language I don't understand, surrounded by characters who keep whispering, 'Just write something!'"

Explore Different Perspectives

Exploring your problems from different perspectives involves imagining how various versions of yourself—past, present, or even future—would approach and react to the situation. This technique adds depth and humor by contrasting different viewpoints and experiences.

Importance in Comedy

- **Variety of Insights:** Different perspectives reveal diverse attitudes and reactions, uncovering humorous contradictions or revelations.

- **Character Exploration:** Imagining how different versions of yourself would handle a problem allows for character-driven comedy, where each perspective brings its own comedic style and quirks.
- **Empathy and Connection:** By examining problems from multiple angles, comedians can connect with a broader audience who may relate to different phases of personal growth and change.

In her special "Elder Millennial," Iliza Shlesinger explores dating problems from various perspectives, including acting out scenarios as if she were a peacock approaching dating. This playful shift in perspective adds humor by juxtaposing human behavior with animal instincts.

Jokes from Different Perspectives

- **Current Self:** "When I face a crowd, my current self feels like a deer caught in headlights, except the headlights are actually the audience's eyes, and they're all blinking in unison."
- **Childhood Self:** "As a kid, public speaking was like being asked to perform magic tricks in front of the entire class—I'd freeze up, forget all my tricks, and end up pulling a rabbit out of a hat that was clearly empty."
- **Imaginary Future Self:** "In the future, I imagine public speaking will be as effortless as giving TED talks in zero gravity, where every word floats perfectly into place, and the audience applauds with jetpacks."

Use Callbacks and Running Gags

Callbacks and running gags in comedy involve referencing a specific joke, theme, or problem throughout a performance, creating continuity and allowing comedians to build on earlier humor for added comedic effect.

Importance in Comedy

- **Continuity and Cohesion:** Callbacks create a sense of continuity in a comedy set, tying together disparate jokes or anecdotes into a cohesive narrative.

- **Enhanced Humor:** Each callback can build on previous references, adding layers of humor as the audience recognizes and recalls earlier jokes.
- **Audience Engagement:** Running gags engage the audience by inviting them to follow along with recurring themes or jokes, rewarding their attention and participation.

Mike Birbiglia's "Sleepwalk with Me" integrates his experiences with a sleep disorder throughout the entire show, using callbacks to revisit and expand on the central theme of his sleepwalking adventures. Each callback deepens the audience's understanding and enjoyment of his comedic storytelling.

Brainstorming Callbacks

- **Callback 1:** "You know you're procrastinating when you're reorganizing your entire desk setup for the third time this week instead of starting that project. Maybe if I arrange my pens by color, inspiration will magically strike."
- **Callback 2:** "Remember that time I tried to convince myself that watching YouTube videos about productivity hacks was actually a productive use of my time? I'm pretty sure I learned more about how to color-code my to-do lists than actually checking anything off."
- **Callback 3:** "I once made a detailed schedule with five-minute intervals to maximize productivity. It lasted exactly one day before I realized I spent more time updating the schedule than doing the actual tasks."
- **Callback 4:** "I tried setting multiple alarms to wake up early and tackle my to-do list. Turns out, hitting snooze on five alarms just means I start my day with a stressful race against time, trying to catch up with the morning I planned hours ago."
- **Callback 5:** "At this point, my procrastination has become so advanced, I've convinced myself that waiting until the last minute is a strategic decision, like a master chess player waiting for the perfect move. Except, instead of a brilliant checkmate, I end up scrambling to finish in a frenzy."

Find the Funny in the Solution Attempts

Finding humor in solution attempts involves examining the often humorous or unexpected ways people try to solve their problems, highlighting the contrast between intentions and outcomes.

Importance in Comedy

- **Absurdity in Efforts:** The gap between intended solutions and actual outcomes can be fertile ground for comedy, revealing human quirks and misconceptions.
- **Relatable Situations:** Everyone has tried unconventional or humorous methods to solve problems, making these anecdotes universally amusing.
- **Reflection and Acceptance:** Laughing at our attempts to solve problems acknowledges our imperfections and fosters self-acceptance through humor.

Gary Gulman's comedy often explores his attempts to deal with personal challenges, such as depression, in hilariously inventive ways. His bit about trying to "depression-proof" his apartment with a weighted blanket and a sun lamp turns a serious topic into a laugh-out-loud moment by exaggerating the absurd lengths he goes to find relief.

Solution Attempts

- **Attempt 1:** "I tried to eat healthier by stocking up on kale and quinoa, but then I discovered that kale tastes like grass and quinoa feels like tiny alien eggs in my mouth."
  - **Funny Aspect:** "Apparently, my taste buds are not on board with the whole 'superfood' movement."
- **Attempt 2:** "I bought a juicer thinking I'd start each day with a fresh kale-spinach smoothie. It ended up becoming a decoration on my kitchen counter, mocking me with its untouched pristine condition."
  - **Funny Aspect:** "I spend more time cleaning the juicer than actually using it. Who knew vegetables could be so messy?"
- **Attempt 3:** "I downloaded a meal planning app that promised to make cooking healthy meals a breeze. Instead, it made me

feel guilty every time I ordered pizza instead of following its meticulously planned recipes."
- o **Funny Aspect:** "My phone judging my dinner choices was not the motivation I needed."

Turning your problems into punchlines is both an art and a therapeutic process. It requires vulnerability, creativity, and a willingness to look at your struggles from new angles. Remember, the goal isn't to trivialize your problems, but to find the universal humor in them that can connect you with your audience.

As you practice these techniques, you'll likely find that some work better for you than others. Develop your unique style of problem-to-punchline alchemy. And remember, even if a joke doesn't land perfectly, the act of transforming your struggles into comedy is valuable in itself.

Structuring Your Set for Maximum Impact

A well-structured comedy set is like a perfectly orchestrated symphony – each element builds upon the last, creating a cohesive and impactful experience for the audience. Whether you're performing a five-minute open mic or a full hour special, the structure of your set can make or break your performance. Let's dive into the art and science of crafting a comedy set that leaves your audience wanting more.

The Importance of a Strong Opening

Your opening is crucial – it sets the tone for your entire set and gives the audience their first impression of you as a performer. The opening joke or statement sets the tone for your set, signaling to the audience what kind of humor they can expect from you. It grabs the audience's attention and establishes a connection early on, helping to build rapport and engagement.

Start with a strong joke, but not necessarily your absolute best. You want to leave room to escalate the laughter throughout your set.

Ellen DeGeneres often opens her shows with quick, punchy observational humor to immediately engage the audience. In one special, she starts with, "It's great to be here. I like to start my shows by saying something that everyone in the audience can relate to. So... we're all gonna die."

Establishing Your Persona

Early in your set, you need to establish who you are and what kind of comedy the audience can expect. Include a joke or anecdote early on that encapsulates your unique comedic perspective or style. This helps define your persona and sets expectations for the audience.

Your opening joke should reflect your persona clearly. Whether it's dark, observational, whimsical, or satirical, it should resonate with your overall comedic approach.

Anthony Jeselnik establishes his dark and shocking persona right from the start. For instance, opening with a line like "My girlfriend makes me want to be a better person... so I can get a better girlfriend" immediately sets the tone for his edgy and provocative style of humor.

The Flow: Building Momentum

Creating a natural flow in your comedy set is essential for keeping the audience engaged and connected from start to finish:

1. **Logical Progression**: Each joke or bit should logically lead to the next. This can be achieved through thematic connections, callbacks, or transitioning from one topic to another smoothly.
2. **Using Segues**: Segues are crucial for seamless transitions between topics. These can range from simple connecting phrases to witty remarks that bridge one joke or story to the next.

John Mulaney is known for his subtle and often humorous segues that tie different topics together. For example, transitioning from a bit about his dog to one about his wife with the line, "Speaking of bitches..." demonstrates his ability to maintain flow while adding a comedic twist that fits his persona.

Varying Joke Structures and Rhythms

Variety in joke structures and rhythms keeps your set dynamic and prevents it from becoming predictable:

1. **Mixing Joke Types**: Alternate between different joke structures such as one-liners, longer anecdotes, act-outs, and potentially crowd work if it aligns with your style.
2. **Engaging the Audience**: Different joke structures appeal to different audience preferences and keep them actively listening and laughing throughout your performance.

Dave Chappelle excels in mixing long-form storytelling with sharp one-liners and physical comedy. In "Sticks & Stones," he seamlessly transitions from personal stories and reflections on life to timely and punchy jokes about current events. This variety not only showcases his versatility but also maintains a high level of engagement with the audience.

Building to a Climax

Your set should have a clear arc, building to a high point near the end. Place your strongest material strategically throughout the set, with a concentration of power towards the end.

Hannah Gadsby's "Nanette" is structured like a classic comedy special for the first two-thirds, then builds to an intense, thought-provoking climax that recontextualizes everything that came before.

The Call-Back: Tying It All Together

A call-back in comedy refers to referencing a joke, situation, or element from earlier in your set later on, often in an unexpected or surprising way. Here's how you can effectively use call-backs:

1. **Creating Cohesion**: Call-backs help create a sense of cohesion in your set by linking different parts of your performance together.
2. **Rewarding the Audience**: They reward attentive audience members who remember previous jokes or stories, enhancing their enjoyment of your performance.

3. **Unexpected Contexts**: Use call-backs in unexpected contexts to add humor and surprise. This can involve revisiting a joke's punchline, referencing a character or situation introduced earlier, or even using visual or verbal cues that echo earlier material.

Mike Birbiglia is known for his intricate call-backs. In this show, he references a childhood story about a carnival ride at the very end of the show, bringing the entire narrative full circle. This not only ties together thematic elements but also provides a satisfying conclusion to his performance.

The Rule of Threes in Set Structure

The rule of threes is a principle used in comedy for creating rhythm and emphasis. Here's how it applies to both individual jokes and overall set structure:

Overall Set Structure:

- **Dividing into Segments**: Structure your comedy set into three main segments or acts. Each segment should build upon the previous one, either in intensity, complexity, or thematic development.
- **Creating Flow**: The rule of threes helps maintain a balanced flow in your performance, allowing for variation and progression while keeping the audience engaged.

Bo Burnham's special "Inside" is loosely structured in three acts. The first act explores themes of isolation, the second delves into darker and more introspective themes, and the third acts as a meta-commentary on the special itself and his creative process during lockdown.

Each act in "Inside" builds upon the previous one, offering a deeper exploration of themes and evolving the comedic and emotional journey for the audience.

Crafting a Solid Closing Bit

Your closing bit is crucial as it leaves a lasting impression on your audience. Here are some tips to craft a strong closing:

1. **Tie Back to Themes**: Ideally, your closing bit should reference or tie together themes that have been explored throughout your set. This gives a sense of coherence and completeness to your performance.
2. **End on a Strong Joke**: Finish with a joke that encapsulates your comedic voice and style. This joke should be memorable and ideally provoke strong laughter from the audience.
3. **Call Back to Earlier Material**: Consider calling back to an earlier joke or story in your set. This creates a sense of continuity and can provide a satisfying conclusion by bringing the audience full circle.

Ali Wong often ends her specials with a bold or outrageous statement that embodies the themes she has explored throughout her set. For instance, in "Baby Cobra," she closes with a graphic joke about motherhood, which ties back to her exploration of pregnancy and relationships.

Theming Your Set

Having a thematic approach can greatly enhance the impact and coherence of your comedy set:

1. **Central Theme or Question**: Identify a central theme or question that your jokes and anecdotes revolve around. This theme serves as a guiding principle for structuring your material.
2. **Consistency and Cohesion**: By maintaining a consistent theme, you create a cohesive narrative thread that connects all parts of your performance.

Hasan Minhaj's special is themed around his experiences growing up as a first-generation Indian-American. All his stories and jokes are tied back to this central concept of cultural identity, belonging, and family dynamics. Each joke or anecdote in the set reinforces and elaborates on aspects of Minhaj's personal narrative, offering insights and humor that resonate with the overarching theme.

Crowd Work Integration

Crowd work refers to the improvisational interaction a performer has with the audience during a live show. Here's how you can effectively integrate crowd work into your comedy set:

Planning and Structure:

- **Identify Natural Points**: Plan specific moments in your set where crowd work can naturally fit. This could be after a particularly strong joke, during a lull, or as an opener to engage the audience.
- **Transitions**: Prepare segues that smoothly transition from your prepared material into crowd interaction and back. These transitions ensure that your set remains cohesive and doesn't feel disjointed.

Begin your set with well-rehearsed jokes or stories to establish your comedic rhythm and set the tone. Use audience responses or cues to segue into crowd work. Dave Attell is known for his ability to seamlessly weave in spontaneous interactions with the audience while maintaining control over the show.

Always have a pathway back to your prepared material. This can be through callbacks, structured segues, or returning to the next joke in your set list.

The "Chunk" Approach

The chunk approach involves organizing your comedy set into thematic or topical segments. This method helps with memorization, flow, and audience engagement:

Organizational Strategy

- **Thematic Grouping**: Group jokes, anecdotes, or topics into cohesive "chunks" based on common themes or subjects. For example, you might have chunks on family life, current events, or observations about daily routines.
- **Clear Transitions**: Ensure each chunk has a clear transition between them. This could be a punchline that leads into the next topic, a brief segue, or a thematic connection that ties them together.
- **Memorization Aid**: Structuring your set into chunks aids in memorization because you can mentally categorize and recall jokes more easily based on the chunk they belong to.

Jerry Seinfeld often organizes his stand-up routines into clear thematic chunks. For instance, he might have a section focusing on social etiquette, followed by one on personal quirks, and another on observations about daily life.

This approach allows for a balanced flow of humor and variety within the set. Each chunk can offer a different perspective or comedic style while maintaining coherence. By addressing different topics, you can engage a broader range of audience members who may relate to different aspects of your material.

Structuring a comedy set is as much an art as it is a science. While these techniques provide a solid foundation, the best structure for your set will depend on your personal style, the type of material you're presenting, and the specific audience you're performing for.

Remember, the goal of structure is to enhance your comedy, not constrain it. A well-structured set should feel natural and effortless to the audience, even though you've put considerable thought into its construction.

As you develop your set, don't be afraid to experiment with different structures. What works on paper might not work on stage, and vice versa. Use open mics and smaller shows to test different arrangements of your material.

Create 60 Minutes of New Material

To keep their material fresh for long sets and tours, comedians must consistently generate new jokes, bits, and full routines. This section will demonstrate the process of creating a full hour of new comedy material from start to finish. Each segment will include sample jokes, stories, or bits to provide a concrete example of fresh material. Topics covered will include joke writing techniques, developing character-based premises, crafting narrative bits, and structuring the overall set. By breaking down an hour-long set creation process, readers can gain insight into how working professionals develop substantial amounts of new comedy material.

Opening Jokes (5 minutes)

A strong opener is key to grabbing audience attention immediately. Here is a sample opener with 3 one-liner jokes:

- "Hey, has anyone else noticed grocery stores playing music you don't want to have sex to? Like, I don't need Barry Manilow killing the mood while I'm grabbing condoms."
- "My girlfriend's into some kinky stuff in bed. The other night she asked me to dress up as myself and just lie there quietly."
- "Speaking of kinky, I saw an ad the other day for a threesome cruise. I say if you're gonna go, bring an extra set of clothes - the last thing you want is to run into your neighbors after."

Premise: Online Dating (10 minutes)

Online dating provides endless material. Here is a longer bit exploring catfishing encounters:

"So I've been doing some online dating, which has led to some odd situations. Like this one woman who used 10 year old photos on her profile. When we met in person, a friendly neighborhood opossum greeted me instead. I tried to let her down easy - I said 'I'm just not physically attracted to you OR marsupials.'"

"Or the time I matched with a woman who claimed to love hiking and the outdoors. Our first date was at a Starbucks. When I asked what happened to all our mutual interests, she said 'Oh, I just say that stuff to trick guys into meeting me. I actually hate nature and only leave the house for pumpkin spice lattes.'"

Premise: Family Dynamics (10 minutes)

Families provide an untapped mine of relatable absurdity. Here's a character piece about a eccentric uncle:

"You gotta meet my Uncle Eddie. He's one of a kind. For Christmas last year, his gift to me was a VHS tape he recorded of himself waterskiing. No explanation, no note - just a unlabeled tape of a 60 year old man shakily skiing across a murky pond. Of course I had to watch it. And it was riveting cinema, let me tell you. The choreography, the tension, the climax - it had it all. Now every holiday, I'm on edge waiting to see what homemade masterpiece Uncle Eddie has in store next."

Story: A Day at the Park (10 minutes)

Long-form stories allow for narrative arcs. Here's one about a disastrous day at the playground:

"So me and the kids decided to spend a Saturday at the park. What could go wrong, right? Well, first my two year old falls face-first into the wood chips trying to climb the ladder up the slide. Then my four year old tries to rescue a baby bird that fell out of a tree - with her teeth. And don't even get me started on the melted down tantrum my toddler threw when it started raining ice cream. By the time we left, I was wondering if CPS would let me adopt a new, less terrifying family at the playground."

Character: The Annoying Gym Member (5 minutes)

Some of the best bits come from exaggerating actual people. Here's one about a chatty gym regular:

"Hey, has anyone joined a new gym lately? Let me tell you about Brad, the most enthusiastic personal trainer you'll ever dread. Every morning at 6am like clockwork, he finds me on the elliptical to give me a play-by-play of his entire weekend. And I mean entire. Every drunken Snapchat, every bites of every meal, every Tinder match - I know more about this guy's life than my own family at this point. The other day I started lying that I was deaf just to get some peace on that damn machine."

Story: My First Stand Up Gig (7 minutes)

All comedians have a story about their initial time on stage. Here's a sample bit recounting a disastrous first show:

"So in my early funny days, I decided to try my hand at the local open mic. I figured how hard could five minutes be, right? Well, I bombed so badly I'm surprised they didn't charge me for emotional damages. Within the first joke, I realized I left my notecards at home so I was just up there sweating in dead silence. And to make matters worse, the guy before me did 25 minutes of brilliant crowd work so the bar was set impossibly high. By the end, I practically had to beg the host not to ban me from ever returning. And trust me, he considered it."

Story: My Short-Lived Music Career (8 minutes)

Turning an eccentric experience into a longer story allows for more jokes. Here's one about trying to start a band:

"So in college, I had this brilliant idea that I was gonna be the next big rockstar. Never mind that I didn't actually play an instrument or know how to sing - I had vision, dammit. After placing an ad on Craigslist, four other delusional dreamers and I formed our garage band. We called ourselves 'Broccoli & Tea' which should give you insight into our combined artistic talents. I'm honestly amazed we survived the three practices it took for us all to admit we should probably stick to day jobs and open mics. Luckily, our one and only show was just for our stoner neighbors who mostly felt bad for us."

Closing (5 minutes)

A strong closing ties off the routine. Here are a couple final jokes:

- "All in all, it's been a weird year finding my comedy footing. But I'm learning that the only way to have a truly memorable first time on stage is to forget your pants."
- "Anyway, thanks for letting me share some stories tonight. I hope I didn't scare you all back into your online dating profiles forever. Unless you're into the opossum types - then you're in luck, I know a guy."

Exercises: Solo Joke-Writing Exercises; Pair Exercises to Workshop and Refine Jokes

Dedicated practice is crucial for any comedian seeking to sharpen their joke writing skills. This article provides professional level solo and collaborative exercises to help take joke crafting abilities to the next level. Solo exercises focus on constraint-based prompts stimulating creativity through limitations. Meanwhile, pair workshops offer invaluable feedback opportunities through structured testing and refinement. These tried-and-true exercises have benefitted countless comedians over the years by facilitating fresh perspectives and iterative improvements. Used regularly, they systematically strengthen comedic muscles leading to polished, crowd-pleasing material.

Solo Joke-Writing Exercises

Crystallizing Humor Economy

Challenging oneself to rigid 3-word joke constraints crystallizes humor in dense, potent gems. Each word carries comedic weight to paint a vivid scene in just a breviloquent triad. Potential for clever absurdity abounds within ultra-miniaturized formats testing efficient joke-crafting skills.

Object-Centered Brainstorming

Selecting an object as the point of departure randomly sparks imagination connecting that prop to various amusing scenarios through diverse jest-based setups. Whether cue cards or curling irons, having a focal non-sequitur center stimulates comedy discovery through its many application potentials as the prime element tying 25 jokes together.

Tongue-Tangling Triggers

Purposefully clumsy collections of alliterative, assonantal, or rhyming sounds pairings for punchline-bound setups induce tongue-tied hilarity. Nonsensical sequences stumble delightfully into punch delivering the payoff. Stylized cadences carry jokes innovatively while exercising witty lexicon dexterity through linguistically challenging structures.

Alphabetical Antics

Structuring jokes according to consecutive letters presents a constraint-based challenge. Generating "All bugs can't dance elegantly" would follow "All baboons crave drunken escapades." Forced sequence sparks spontaneous absurdities, wordplay opportunities abound within tight creative confines of alphabetical order. Subsequent zingers require even more comedic dexterity.

Accruing Daily Daubs of Humor

Noting three amusing observations each day from overheard comments or peculiar sights primes comedic lenses. Returning regularly to craft notation into tight, punchy joke format keeps humor skills sharp. Extracting laughter from mundanities makes light of everyday absurdities previously taken for granted. Process tunes capacity to mine mirth from any situation.

Expansive Angular Jest

Extracting humor from a single topic through diverse angles, perspectives or characters within it exercises multi-threaded joke exploration abilities. Whether personal biases, figurative vantages or hyperbolic character viewpoints, joke iteration goes deeper. Practice multi-faceted comedic resonance from various joke prisms related to one nucleus topic, mining overlooked territories of absurd within.

Rearward Revelatory Japes

Rather than standardized setup to punchline trajectory, concocting punchlines then building humorous premises backward surprises with unprecedented inventiveness. Devising a punch then supporting retrospectively introduced joke formulations challenges preconceived patterns. Subverted structures birth fresh takes by reversing formulaic constraints.

Collaborative Pair Exercises

Timed Creativity Catalysis

Partners issue short-timed challenges for high-pressure joke sprints, prohibiting editability unleashes free flow ideas. Uncensored uncorks humor innovation through imposed deadlines, unearthing nuggets requiring polish. Playful competition motivates quantity while cultivating myriad angles meriting later development.

Reciprocal Refinement

Swapping rough chunks elicits line-by-line critiques from allies, noting strengths and outlining areas streamlining impact, flow or element of surprise. Constructive criticism doubles learning; critiquing others' amalgamating received feedback catalyzes growth in both. Iterative exchange polishes each other's potential.

Immediate Live-Action Feedback

Testing partially shaped wit in real time allows identifying phrasing emphasis, pace, or delivery nuances elevating punchlines for audience. Face-to-face try-outs permits spontaneous adjustments enhancing resonance before wide distribution. Timely suggestions from trustworthy companions improve live presentation skills.

Collaborative Creativity Cultivation

Brainstorming combined prompts, then taking turns contributing sole sentences to a mutually built comedic bit relinquishes singular control, fostering novelty through unity. Unpredictable direction sparks humor innovation exceeding any solo efforts. Shared imagination nurtures fresh synergistic visions greater than the sum.

Collective Character Cultivation

Partnering establishes multilayered character backgrounds together - from quirks and goals to hangups introducing comedic knots solved jointly through scenic collaborations. Spinning interconnected character sketches exercises situational hilarity through communicative development exercising complementary creativity. Detail-oriented participation cultivates understanding to authentically voice imagined personas.

Progressive one-upmanship provocations

Spinning in rotation, rapid sample joke presentations issue challenges for the other to instantaneously one-up the last with a witty "yes, and..." variation or superior spin on the same theme. Improvisational escalation exercises competitive instincts fueling spontaneous absurdity elaboration. Stimulating spirited playfulness awakens new joke tangents left undiscovered through individual ideation alone.

Forced Perspective Fruition

Volunteering for societal stereotypes - like helicopter parents, activists, or food snobs - generates debates finding sweet humor through juxtaposed lens exploration. Assuming polarized role extremes identifies comedic opportunities easing tensions between divergent vantages. Broadened outlooks practice enlightened ridicule skewing no one, instead uniting all perspectives in shared absurdity recognition.

Ideation through Imposed Constraints

Limitations like content warnings, genres or cautionary social norms impose constraints paradoxically catalyzing creative problem-solving. Restrictive parameters provoke rebellious perspective-bending yielding rule-questioning bits. Unconventionality exercises lighthearted social commentary craft perceiving comedy's higher purposes beyond base ridicule. Together, imposed creativity cultivation lifts all boats.

Sample Exercises in Action

Here are a few sample exchanges demonstrating exercises in practice:

Daily Observational Jokes

Observation: A toddler dropping her ice cream

Joke 1: "Saw a little girl drop her ice cream cone. The look on her face went from sad to angry in 1.5 seconds."

Joke 2: "Nothing prepares you to witness a child's first 'This is why we can't have nice things' meltdown after dropping an ice cream."

Collaborative Writing

Prompt: Grocery store

Person 1: An anxious man paced up and down the aisles of the grocery store.

Person 2: His shopping list was so long it trailed behind him, getting covered in spilled soup cans.

Person 1: At checkout, he frantically tried to recall everything he needed as 50 items scanned.

One Topic, Many Angles

Topic: Vacation

Kid's POV: "Dad said the car ride would be fun. He lied - I had to listen to 'The Best of Classical Gas' for 12 hours."

Parent's POV: "I thought a road trip would be quality family time. Now plotting how to dispose of three whiny humans without evidence."

Tourist's POV: "Five star TripAdvisor review didn't mention resort doubles as mosquito factory. Send antidote asap!"

Live Workshopping

Comedian: "You guys, airport security is getting out of hand. I got pulled aside for a random check and the TSA agent found..."

Crowd: "A rubber duck full of hummus!"

Comedian: "Hey, not a bad tag. Let me try that punchline... They found a rubber duck full of hummus! Thanks for the suggestion."

As shown, these exercises stretch comedic muscles through limitations facilitating novel connections and impromptu collaboration refining material mutually. Repeated practice strengthens skills through constraints harnessing the unexpected.

Tips for Effective Joke Crafting Sessions

- Set a timer to 15-20 minutes keeping sharp focus
- Maintain positive, constructive critiques avoiding attacks

- Be receptive to alternate perspectives fueling your own growth
- Celebrate achievements large and small motivating continued exploration
- Most importantly, have fun! Laughter lubricates the creative process

Regular application of solo prompts and collaborative workshops systematically cultivate any comedian's joke writing prowess. Over time, comedic instincts sharpen through dedication to the craft empowering comics to delight audiences with consistently tight, crowd pleasing material. Committed practice using varied exercises systematically strengthens creative chops.

PART 2
MASTERING PERFORMANCE TECHNIQUES

CHAPTER 3

MASTERING PERFORMANCE TECHNIQUES

While having polished material is important, stand-up success hinges on effective live delivery. This chapter focuses on the crucial performance techniques that transform comedy routines from simply written jokes into memorable experiences for audiences. Whether navigating the challenges of nervous energy, commanding stage presence, or eliciting engaged crowd interactions, mastering the performative elements requires dedication to the craft. The following sections will provide comedians guidance on vital skills like timing, vocal control, body language, and receiving audience feedback - all of which factor into fully captivating live crowds night after night. With dedicated practice applying these proven techniques, any comic can elevate their on-stage abilities to dynamic professional levels.

Overcoming Stage Fright

Vulnerability to stage fright is common for performers, yet can debilitate if left unaddressed. This section aims to demystify the experience and provide tools for comedians to effectively manage nerves. From understanding the biological roots of stage fright to developing practical techniques, readers gain empowerment over what was once paralyzing. With guidance on exposure therapy, mental preparation, harnessing nerves productively and adjusting perspective, anyone can transform fright into excited anticipation. Regularly facing fears strengthens comedic confidence enabling comics to fully connect with crowds through relaxed, authentic delivery. With dedication to the outlined methods, performance anxiety need no longer hold comics back from their full potential.

Understanding the Physiology

The Evolutionary Root

Stage fright activates the same fight-or-flight response our ancestors needed for genuine threats in their environment. Faced with potential dangers like predators, adrenaline and cortisol enabled the body to either confront or quickly escape perceived risks. This physiological reaction was adaptive for survival in ancestral times.

The Misattributed Threat

However, in modern performance contexts, there is no true physical danger being signaled by the body's triggers. Events like taking the stage provide no risk of bodily harm. Yet the primitive brain interprets biological alarm signs like racing heart or butterflies as indicating threat, even when in a safe setting.

Understanding the Physiological Reaction

By recognizing stage fright merely stems from an evolutionary hangover misattributing performance as threatening, excessive fear can be mitigated. Once comedians comprehend their biology's role in producing symptoms aimed to aid harm avoidance long ago, they no longer overestimate potential risks. Performance triggers the same instinctive mechanisms, but without genuine cause for alarm.

Calming the Primitive Response

Armed with this knowledge, comedians learn to soothe their primal reactions by reassuring the unconscious that they are secure. Reminding oneself their biology misconstrues triggers as harmful, but reality presents no risk, can calm disproportionate threat appraisals. Understanding stage fright's physiological root in fight-or-flight demystifies and thus alleviates anxiety.

Embracing Vulnerability

Where initial instincts may encourage wrestling nerves into submission, a wiser approach accepts their valid role as signalling deep care and commitment to the craft. A thoughtful mindset shift reframing perceived "fear" as productive "excitement" efficiently leverages energy normally experienced as paralyzing. All legendary performers undoubtedly felt butterflies when starting out. Viewing jitters in this positive light empowers them to propel rather than cripple presentations through enthusiastic channeling.

It is critically important for emerging comedians to extend compassion first towards themselves as works-in-progress honing formidable skills, rather than harshly demanding flawless, unfeeling perfection. Nerves are universal, yet viewing them with gentle understanding as expected parts of the process rebuilds anticipated fragility into strength. While continually enhancing abilities, keeping present focus on steady growth nurtures well-being over distress. Accepting vulnerability as bravely human allows authentically bonding with audiences through shared imperfections highlighting commonalities over perceived separations.

Exposure Therapy

Beginning with Babysteps

New comedians can start with low-intensity exposures like recording practice sets alone or sharing jokes with trusting loved ones. These minimal perceived judgment environments allow acclimating to performance feelings in safe spaces with support. Repeated baby steps, with frequent but brief exposures, accustom the body and brain to distress signs in a controlled manner. This graduated exposure prevents being overwhelmed and trains one's threat response that there is nothing truly threatening occurring.

Building Confidence in Comfort Zones

Regularly performing at open mics or local venues with supportive crowds who are not there to harshly critique provides an especially secure space. These low-stakes shows, often multiple times per week, clearly demonstrate each time through experience that the dreaded feared outcome consistently fails to occur. Realizing time and again that the anxiety proved entirely unwarranted greatly boosts one's coping skills and makes them more willing and able to face slightly larger and broader audiences.

Gradually Expanding Comfort Boundaries

Once some stability is attained through frequent safe exposures, one can cautiously push their boundaries a bit at a time by volunteering for earlier time slots requiring engaging the audience when they may be less warmed up, or by intentionally trying out new or riskier material that goes slightly beyond one's tested comfort zone. Continued exposure through these managed small step-ups helps further train down the threat response over repeated exposures showing there is nothing truly dangerous. Steady advances harness anxiety's inability to self-perpetuate when one is never harmed.

Reinforcing Success through Mastery

As more challenging shows are faced and experienced as successful rather than threatening due to gradual exposure, drawing repeated confidence from these mastery experiences is important. Intentionally recalling prior successes, no matter how small, serves to train one's memory to more easily and readily access these positive rather than feared results of performance. Repeated reflection on the accumulated proof, through many exposures over time, that performance poses absolutely no real danger ultimately conquers the subconscious conditioning of threat and frees the comedian's performance from anxiety's unwanted grasp.

Focus Redefining

Emerging comedians can channel anticipatory jitters into pure performance joy by deliberately shifting inner monologue. Visualizing a smiling, supportive crowd hanging on every word redirects scattered thoughts onto enthused connection. Appreciating each fluently delivered line and appreciative laugh as personal wins clears mental clutter. Focusing solely on witty material delivery versus intrusive self-criticism relaxes through positive visualization. With practice, simply cueing an envisioned comedic scenario suffuses the body with energized calm rather than tension.

As skills progress, concentrating exclusively on honing the craft instead of amassing flaws for self-judgment dissolves counterproductive pressures. Positive self-talk acknowledges every stepping stone forward versus perceived imperfections hindering. Even experienced veterans envision receptive audiences, mentally blocking all distractions to stay fully present. This sharpened focus strengthens confidence by demonstrating each performance tests solely the material, not fragile egos. Ridding mental clutter through visionary relaxation trains the mind for laser-like engagement untainted by doubts.

Pre-Show Rituals

Focusing the Mind Through Breathwork

Simple breathing techniques implemented before walking onstage break the feedback loop of worrying thoughts. Deep inhalations and exhalations oxygenate the body while calming nerves. Counting breaths transfers mental energy from anxieties onto sensation of air entering and leaving the lungs. Over time, the ritual alone becomes soothing.

Empowering Affirmations for Self-Talk

Positive self-affirming notes carry confidence-boosting messages to reread before performances. Phrasing like "I've prepared well and audiences will love my set" redirects inner monologue from doubts onto belief in one's abilities. Customized daily affirmations reprogram anxious assumptions with empowered self-perspectives.

Uplifting Music Shifts Energy

Curated upbeat pre-show playlists match desired energetic state. Fast tempo songs correlate arousal to confidence rather than nerves. Lyrics about rising to challenges reframe performance from threatening to thrilling. Over time, hearing just a song triggers the linked empowered state through classical conditioning of music and mood.

Routinizing Control Over Variables

Consistency in rituals weans focus from controllables like audience reactions onto management of readiness. Performers gain sovereignty over preparation quality rather than outcomes beyond influence. Regular routines become anchors calming through predictable familiarity when stakes feel highest.

Mental Simulation

Prior to vulnerable live appearances, emerging comedians purposefully visualize seamless performances in vivid granular detail through mental simulation. Envisioning calm, composed deliveries just as hoped strengthens nerves. Replaying highlights from past wins trains the mind to more readily access confident memories rather than obsessing over potential failures. Focusing intently each relaxing vision primes the brain neurochemically for assured projection versus dreading hypothetical disasters, keeping fragile minds from spiraling endlessly. Over time, mental prep becomes nearly as impactful as real experiences.

As skill builds, mental imagery evolves into an invaluable daily practice reinforcing fearless mindsets. Experienced comics convincingly envision interactional flourishes, customized facial expressions matching each witticism, and appreciative crowd responses programmed. Simulating mastery instills renewed motivation facing fresh obstacles. Whether reliving a triumphal hour or fantasizing innovations, mental rehearsal maintains composure by occupying overthinking minds with exciting creative stimulation. This focused calm supersedes panic, optimizing both memory and performance when visualization transforms anticipated dread into eager anticipation.

Support Systems

The Immense Value of Empathetic Allies

Being interconnected with a community of other comedic performers who fully comprehend both the immense struggles and enormous rewards of this craft in a genuinely understanding manner provides remarkable value. Fellow comics can empathetically grasp the depths of fears, humiliations of failures, and heights of triumphs in a uniquely insightful way that most outsiders simply cannot. Having this level of true empathy from others walking the same path nourishes confidence by reminding that challenges are universally part of the process, and that support is always readily available.

Camaraderie Unequivocally Conquers Anxiety

Knowing that unpredictable open mic audiences will be faced boldly side-by-side with allied peers who are eagerly prepared to provide encouragement and solidarity makes the high-pressure setting exponentially more manageable to withstand. Performing unitedly as a cohesive front against potential nerves and jitters allows redirecting vast amounts of energy normally spent worrying and spinning fearful hypotheticals alone. Bonding powerfully through sharing the difficulties of this shared journey imbues comfort in recognizing that even potential "bombing" on stage feels eminently survivable with trusted companions afterward still ready to lift one's spirit.

Benchmarking Achievements Against Peers

Observing in detail the diverse experiences of fellow comics, encompassing both enormous triumphs and crushing failures, offers indispensable perspective in grounding outlandish anxieties and unreasonable visions of potential downfalls. Regular communal check-ins permit sharing continually accumulated lessons expanding everyone's collective toolkit of wisdom and insight over lengthening time. Witnessing allies successfully meet noteworthy milestones along the path feels tangibly within reach, fueling unmatched motivation. Valuable advice easily inspires emulation of demonstrably successful techniques and strategies.

Relying Upon a Formidable Safety Net

Recognizing that a robust, far-reaching comedy-based social network exists provides calming reassurance alleviating excessive stakes when boldly trying out works-in-progress material. Allied peers steadfastly serve as a vital, formidable system easing ever-present stressors through constructive critiques, generous sharing of plentiful opportunities, and joyous commiseration as comforting support whenever needed. This safety net liberates comedians to embrace experimentation unfettered.

Post-Show Reflection

After each performance experience, emerging comics acknowledge there is progress yet to be made, not perfection demanded. With self-applause and gratitude for the sheer bravery exhibited alone, post-show reflection shifts focus from flaws towards wins. Dedicated journaling thoroughly explores lessons learned, pinch-points necessitating adjustment, and moments bringing unexpected thrills that could be bottled. This structured reflection discourages defaulting into harsh self-criticism or obsessive reliving of perceived failures. Cataloging incremental skills sharpening affirms the inspiring journey underway.

As positive reflections accumulate, performance anxiety's powerful grip gradually loosens its hold. Looking back through journals filled with small triumphs, comedians witness concrete evidence how far nerves have already been retrained. Material and comportment improvements become abundantly clear over dozens of shows tracked systematically. This documented proof of steady competence building satisfies skeptical minds wherever doubt tries planting its flag. Over time, the mountain of evidence shows fears are misaligned, confidence affirmed, and ability to embrace industry risks enriched through self-aware practice and celebration of continual strides forward.

Cognitive Restructuring

Emerging performers can challenge sabotaging automatic thoughts like "I'll certainly freeze up" through dedicated cognitive restructuring. When unhelpful assumptions arise, they are deliberately replaced with realistic optimism statements repeated patiently. For example, acknowledging prior shows where presentation continued fluently despite nerves recalibrates fearful perspectives. With practice, positive self-talk counters internal scripts of destined failure until the mind more readily believes in innate abilities instead of reflexively doubting. Over time, once-ingrained negative thought patterns lose power through targeted challenging and persistent substitution with empowering alternatives.

As skills develop further, anticipating diverse performance scenarios with problem-focused coping replaces avoidance. With experience, imagined stumbles prompt revised statements like "Even if that line tanks, I'll roll with it smoothly" rather than catastrophic predictions. Realizing adaptation skills multiplied shows anticipated "what if" scenarios need altering to match current competencies. Confidence grows recognizing most feared hypotheticals rarely emerge, while preparation readies for any variances calmly. With dedicated cognitive efforts, automatic thoughts transform from a hindrance into hopeful allies fostering fearless experimentation.

Using Jitters Productively

Channeling Adrenaline into Intensity

The chemical rush of stage fright flooding the body with adrenaline and cortisol can be channeled positively. Rather than anxiously fidgeting, comedians learn to laser-focus mental energy and convert physiology into intensely engaged powerful eye contact and vocal projection, fueling enthusiastic live connection with listeners.

Leveraging Rattled Vocal Patterns

Tensely rapid, staccato speech sometimes stemming from rattled nerves is not necessarily a flaw if recognized and leaned into. With practice, comedians realize fast talking stemming from stage jitters can seamlessly blend into and fuel verbal escalations within rapid-fire joke forms, translating typically perceived weakness triumphantly.

Mastering Unpredictable Energies

Where some performers crumble before shifting energies, advanced comedians train mind-body connections to expertly ride waves of naturally unpredictable arousal. They leverage potentially rattling sensations to energize movements, inflections, and sudden segues between topics. Competence wielding variable energies strengthens confidence in abilities to roll with any presentation element.

Strength from Embracing Vulnerability

By acknowledging jitters yet sincerely presenting despite them, comedians show courage embracing perceived flaws. This vulnerability becomes admirable authenticity when used empowering connection through shared human experiences. Performance strengths arise from facing fears, as transformed butterflies amplify artistry negotiating unpredictable conditions.

Acceptance and Self-Compassion

Rather than harshly demanding that performance anxiety vanishes immediately or seeing any nervousness as a terrible personal flaw, comedians must accept with wisdom and patience that overcoming deeply embedded challenges naturally takes significant time and repeated faced exposures. Small victories, like delivering a punchline despite butterflies, should be celebrated while recognizing true progress happens gradually through the journey. Unrealistic expectations that exert pointless pressure and judgment, suggesting success somehow proves inherent worth, must be replaced with gentle understanding.

Learning to effectively manage nerves is a process that accepts setbacks paired with triumphs will occur. Steady persistence and self-kindness, which motivate continued efforts, ease the arduous pressure this craft places upon oneself. Only through self-compassion does one remain inspired along the fulfilling yet lifelong adventures of refining bold artistry while building coping skills against doubts. Progress happens gradually when supported by patience and compassion serving as motivational allies, whereas harshness risks fueling exhaustion. With kindness as a guide, comedians overcome challenges by celebrating strides made each day rather than fixation on a destination still distant.

Maintaining Perspective

Beyond any one show lie fulfillment, community and laughter-related rewards worth short-term vulnerabilities. Balancing longer-term passions with present imperfections reduces performance to a supportive act versus a judgment of self-worth. Life exists beyond outcomes.

Through dedicated practice applying these evidenced techniques, entertainers command not just material but also sensations once crippling. Overcoming performance fears cultivates strength and poise enabling comics to gift authentic joy. With compassion motivating continued growth, no challenge defeats those embracing learned methods for channeling jitters' gift of energy where it serves artistry and souls along life's stages. Courage arises from consistently facing what one fears, not avoiding it.

Developing Confidence and Stage Presence

Powerful stage presence captivates audiences and elevates any performance. While experience builds comfort over time, focused development accelerates progress. This section provides techniques for strengthening comedic confidence and authoritative stage manners through mindset adjustments and skills training. With guidance on mental preparation, body language mastery, vocal projection and charismatic delivery, performers can conquer nerves and command rooms authentically. Regular practice applying these methods systematically cultivates a magnetic stage presence transporting crowds through relaxed command of one's full potential.

Overhauling Limiting Mindsets

Identifying Root Narratives

Emerging comics must identify the root internal narratives fueling persistent self-doubt, such as distortions like "I'm inadequate" or "I don't belong on stage." Pinpointing where these tapes originated and how they have manifested over time provides clarity on thought patterns to target. Journaling prompts excavating past experiences potentially rationalizing present reservations releases bottlenecks blocking bold expression.

Refuting Limiting Beliefs

Once unhelpful root narratives are uncovered, comics deliberatively refute each assumed flaw with objective logic. For example, noting perseverance and continual skill development outweigh perceived imperfections rejects doubts as unfounded. Repetition of empowering statements like "I am talented and original" in front of a mirror helps visualize possessing inherent worth assumed for so long. With dedication, outdated scripts of being unworthy fall away incapable of still finding purchase, eliminated at the source before contributing further to stifled potential.

Ownership Through Presence

Develop pre-show rituals to center your energy onto your craft rather than anxieties. Deep breathing exercises, purposeful body movements like stretches or strides across the stage, and upbeat music through headphones help shift your mindset. Envision commanding the space through visualization techniques like mentally walking the stage confidently. See yourself emanating a welcoming, enthusiastic aura that attracts the audience into a shared experience with you. Drinks of water keep the voice primed for projection. Outwardly direct your energy through focused preparation so that nerves do not inwardly consume potential. Pre-show affirmations customized to your process reinforce intrinsic qualities like courage, humor and soulfulness. Ownership comes from possessing inner strength projected without to engage fully with each moment and attendee. Presence emerges from internal resources outwardly gifted through one's authentic expression.

Body Language Basics

- **Powerful Posture:** To embody confidence, stand tall with squared shoulders relaxed and pulled back along with an erect stance. This "power pose" exudes self-assured control and signals you are approachable. Maintain this body language as you move around to welcome and include everyone in the room.

- **Inclusive Eye Contact:** Make intentional eye contact with all in attendance using your peripheral vision as well as direct eye contact. Slowly scan the room to spread your welcoming energy far and wide. Maintain visual connections to enhance engagement. This shows your attentive presence and invites participation from all perspectives.
- **Congruent Nonverbal Communication:** Pair your confident body language with facial expressions, gestures and mannerisms that match the tone of your spoken words. For example, smiling subtly and using palm-revealing gestures conveys welcome humor. Facing others directly head-on when interacting shows attentive listening. Mimicry of engaged listeners further bonds the group. Together, congruent verbal and nonverbal cues cement your charismatic leadership.

Charismatic Facial Expressions

Smiling naturally and making approachable expressions puts others at ease through friendliness.

Eye Contact and Energy

Make frequent eye contact with different areas of the audience to involve everyone. Scan the room with energetic and expressive eyes. Convey your passion and enthusiasm for your craft through your facial expressions and eye contact.

Vocal Inflection Matches Face

Allow your facial expressions, eyebrow movements and smiles to match the inflections and emphasis in your voice. A contemplative look can enhance a serious point while a smirk accents cheeky humor. Voice and face should be congruent for maximum impact.

Micro-Adjustments

Make micro-adjustments with your eyebrows, eyes and mouth even between jokes to seamlessly transition emotional themes. Subtle expression tweaks keep the audience engaged as you shift topics or build comedic arcs. Fine-tune your facial control for fluid transitions.

Authentic Emotions

Rely on naturally occurring emotions rather than exaggerated or inauthentic-seeming expressions. Your genuine reactions and responses will resonate more sincerely. Discover emotive range that plays to your authentic comic style.

Welcoming Smiles

Smile naturally and make approachable facial expressions to put others at ease through radiating friendliness. A subtle smile signals you are open and relaxed. Your natural smiles will be contagious and help the audience feel comfortable.

Emotive Storytelling

Employ a full range of facial expressions beyond just smiles to engage audiences on deeper levels beyond just words. Use your eyebrows, eyes and overall expressions to succinctly tell stories through your face alone. Make subtle "micro-expressions" to keep story threads intriguing as you move between segments or jokes. Harness the power of nonverbal communication through your face.

Vocal Variety and Projection

Tonal Storytelling

Modulate your vocal tones to add color and dimension to your storytelling. Vary pitch, pace and volume intentionally. Using vocal variety will keep listeners engaged as if in intimate conversation. Project your voice energetically enough that everyone can hear each nuanced detail.

Rising and Falling Emotion

Match your vocal energy to where the audience is emotionally. Convey comedy and pathos authentically by allowing your voice to rise for anticipatory moments and fall for resolution. Use your voice to emphasize climactic points dramatically. Strength comes from voicing your authentic self without reservation.

Presence Through Projection

Ensure your whole audience can hear you by projecting your voice powerfully from your diaphragm. Fill the entire room so that even those furthest away experience your presence fully. Match the acoustics by adjusting your vocal power and tone appropriately for each venue.

Authentic Body Movement

Own the Stage

Move freely across the entire stage without unnecessary fidgeting or filling space with meaningless movement. Convey an ease that is authentic and natural to your individual performance style. Plant yourself in strategic areas to anchor different segments of your set. Own every inch of the stage space assuredly.

Gestures That Enhance

Purposefully incorporate body language, gestures and facial expressions into your storytelling to bring visual dimension. Let movements blossom rhythmically in synchrony with your tonality for maximum impact. Anchor audiences viscerally into climactic moments through body language grounded in the rhythm of your presentation. Discover physical comedy flares unique to your voice and perspective.

Crowd Interactions

Leading with Call-and-Response

Cultivate a collaborative dynamic by smoothly incorporating call-and-response, selective Q&A or playful banter into your set where appropriate. Read the energy of the room and invite participation judiciously. Display confidence guiding interactive moments that enhance, rather than detract from, the comedy crafted.

Rooted Security in Improvisation

With command of scenarios and material, allow space for improvisational skills to emerge within set parameters. Riff confidently off audience prompts rooted in the security of your comedic perspective. Channels shifts in energy or unexpected interactions into the experience smoothly rather flexibility. Authority shows through self-assuredly sharing co-leadership of the journey.

Facilitating a Shared Experience

View your role as a facilitator helping cultivate laughter and joy together with all present. Acknowledge individuals while keeping relation to the collective spirit. Command leadership through confidence including all as co-creators in vignettes sparking merriment for the room as one. Camaraderie develops from masters guiding participatory good times side by side.

Authenticity Over Perfection

Letting go of striving for perfection and worrying excessively over potential mistakes allows your true authentic self and raw charisma to shine through unafraid. While dedicated practice over time refines your material and abilities, making them instinctive, each show or presentation is still a work in progress. By relaxing into your imperfections with ease and acknowledging your humanness, you in fact project a deep sense of relatability that sincerely cements connections with your audience. Those who watch will appreciate your authenticity rather than judging you for minor errors. With security founded within in your genuine self and craft, sharing vulnerably and honestly from that place of rooted strength will serve you far better than forcing rigidity. Each experience is an opportunity for positive growth, and audiences will embrace the realities of the journey when it is lived with transparent conviction on stage.

By refining these techniques, performers actualize magnetic stage presences fully captivating crowds through authentic interactions. Regular adherence progressively builds a command of self projecting self-assuredness attracting listeners into rich story worlds. Ultimately, stage presence stems from establishing internal frameworks permitting liberated expression of artistry exactly as each shares it best – with tranquil authority seated within. Continued focus cultivates this comfort accessing full potentials through welcoming of imperfection.

The Art of Timing and Delivery

Just as timing is everything in comedy, so too is delivery the vehicle propelling jokes home. This section focuses on nuanced skills like meaningful pauses, transition smoothness, pace manipulation and emphasis impacting every performance aspect. With guidance on techniques like punchline delivery, call-and-response interactivity and instinctive improvisation, comedians can elevate timing and delivery mastery. Regular practice applying consistent timing principles systematically strengthens the instinctive rhythms connecting comic and crowd. Committed students can transform delivery from an afterthought to comedy's pulse compelling full engagement.

The Power of Pauses

- **Build Anticipation:** Strategic, well-timed pauses after a Setup or just before the Punchline build crucial anticipation and heighten the comedy payoff. Leave just enough space to tease and tempt what's coming next without giving it away. A breath or two can work better than full lengthy pauses.
- **Consider Context:** Calibrate the perfect duration of pauses based on the content, context and energy of the specific set or segment. What works best is contingent on joke composition, performance style and audience responsiveness. Too short or too long risks losing the flow or focus.
- **Just Enough Suspense:** Pausing with precise purpose keeps the crowd metaphorically and literally on the edge of their seats, eagerly awaiting your next words. Factor in just enough suspense or tease to enhance the comedy, without leaving them hanging so long that interest lapses. Masterful pacing maximizes dramatic effect.

Transition Tenderness

- **Fluid Handoffs:** Fluidly transition between jokes, stories or topics to maintain a coherent flow for the audience. Practiced or improvised "bridges" can link seemingly disjointed bits together cohesively. Smooth handoffs between segments keep the energy level consistent without abrupt breaks in rhythm.

- **Choreographed Segways:** Rehearse transitional techniques that choreographically advance the set enthrallingly from beginning to end. Whether predetermined or impromptu, utilize segues like call-backs, topical tags or interactive buffers that tie the threads of humor end-to-end. Carefully crafted connectivity maintains momentum between belly laughs.
- **Natural Progression:** With practice, connections may arise organically in the moment through allusions, smooth callbacks or topical tags. Develop a rapport and rhythm attuned to audience cues allowing for seamless shifts that progress as a natural scene development would. Laughter begets more laughter through considered flow.

Punchline Precision

Mastering the subtle alchemy of precisely accentuating just the right words within the punchline allows you to instantly deliver the climactic moment with perfect comedic timing. A minor emphasis shift, whether voicing that one pivotal word slightly quicker than the rest of the sentence, increasing vocal volume a hair on the punch, or cleanly enunciating the syllable for extra clarity - these microscopic adjustments seamlessly package and deliver the payoff. By accentuating the punch sharply you bypass having to wait for the audience to cognitively process the build up and simply realize the humorous resolution, instead propelling the laughter immediately. With a well-placed inflection, you receive quick returns on your setup by converting recognition into reaction without lag. Finesse in accentuating punchlines through subtle emphasis yields powerful dividends by optimizing the speed at which you can launch laughs successively. Punchline precision procures rapid-fire reward.

Delivery by Character

- **Distinct Voices and Inflections:** Bring characters to vivid life through distinct voice inflections, accent work or tonal idiosyncrasies that personify their unique personalities. Embodying these vocal stamps adds full dimension especially for recurring figures. Nuanced vocal characterizations keep depictions lively and believable.

- **Relatable through Authentic Embodiment:** Immerse listeners viscerally by fully assuming character personas when inhabiting scenarios. Physical embodiment complements vocal delivery to help transport the audience seamlessly into comedic vignettes seen through that lens. Authentically channeling mentality grounds relatability.
- **Selling through Sympathetic Eyes:** Relate relatable tales through a character's sympathetic eyes leaving impression beyond the direct joke. Giving full substance to archetypes anchors audiences emotionally within settings increasing comedy impact long-term. Voice infuses humanity keeping portrayals colorful set to set.

Interactive Improvisation

- **Feeding off Crowd Energy:** Invite audience participation and call-and-response moments by feeding off their energy through an upbeat, conversational performance rhythm and tone. Your body language and eye contact should signal an open, playful dynamic encouraging responses within predictable beats of the set.
- **Playful Repartee and Collision:** Stimulate chuckles through impromptu, playful repartee and predetermined comedic "collisions" with engaged audience members. Timing these interactions perfectly keeps the spontaneity lively and laughter-inducing versus awkward. Stay light on your toes for loose Improv.
- **Thriving in the Moment:** Rather than fearing unpredictability, relish rolling with serendipitous discoveries emerging alongside attentive crowds. Your ability to authentically listen and think on your feet facilitates bonding over surprises. Build from sparks ignited together through active co-creation.

Delivering Long Form

Executing a truly compelling long form storytelling or observational set requires adept modulation of pacing throughout its various segments, jokes and levels to maintain engagement. Varying delivery speeds across setups, callbacks, tangents and payoffs is key, to surprise listeners and keep their full attention anchored. From drawn out, almost suspensefully slowed builds ups, to succinctly clipped punchlines popping at just the right moment, a full spectrum of tempos across the arc of the material spices up the content and prevents tedium. Layered jokes land with maximum impact too when allowed to breathe differently. Consistently surprising and stimulating the audience through dynamic pace manipulation across the full span is essential to transporting them on a multi-layered comedic journey that feels fresh, alive and thrilling minute after minute rather than plodding stagnantly at a one-note rate. Nuanced manipulation keeps the nuanced narrative rolling along at a naturally engaging pace.

Nailing the Big Finish

Just as a first impression colors a crowd's receptiveness, a standout finale seals the whole experience in their memory long after the show. Craft your closers carefully through rehearsal to deliver culminating jokes or stories with utmost punchline precision and impact. Choreograph precisely whether those final climactic lines will land with breathless rushed climax or poised dramatic draw-out - either way maximize that conclusive laugh. A powerful big finish that sticks the landing will reward audiences with a high to take with them, recalling fondly your delivery and warmth well beyond the show's end. Ensure the savored flavor lingering longest is your timeless comedic timing and style. Nothing leaves a more indelible stamp of your talent than nailing that climactic send off with rehearsed flair giving full due to all who laughed alongside your inspiring journey.

Using Beats Instantaneously

The skilled comedic performer wields even the subtlest physical beats and minuscule motions to instantly punctuate and accentuate the punchlines, climactic moments and nuanced shifts throughout a set. From a deliberately slowed inhale drawing anticipation before unleashing a payoff, to a lingering exhale releasing held tension after the laugh lands, the judicious manipulation of breath precisely punctuates the emotional beats. Mingled with targeted facial micro-expressions subtly communicating varied shades of meaning, eyes remain riveted tracking each intricately crafted shift compelling smiles. Economy and specificity in physical choice enhances vocal delivery, amplifying comedic impact. These microscopic motions marry flawlessly with the oral storytelling to form a harmonious whole greater than the sum of parts. Mastery of the minutiae allows magnification of humor's effect through less proving definitively more in skilled hands.

Adjusting Instinctively

- **Intuitive Attunement:** Intuitively alter your delivery style, tempo, tone and approach to seamlessly match the constantly shifting energy levels within dynamic crowds. Your flexibility to instinctively pick up on and seamlessly adjust to all responsive cues tailors each performance flow uniquely.
- **Guiding with Agility:** Expertly steer shows through natural fluctuations by smoothly speeding up or slowing down delivery based on contextual factors like crowd engagement, transitions between segments or unpredictable disruptions. Your nimble adaptability commands audiences calmly through any ups and downs.
- **Unique Vibe Tuning:** No two rooms or nights are exactly alike, so capture each performance's distinct vibe by delicately modifying your approach with every new environment. Agile tweaking skillfully caters tempo, material selection and interactive elements specifically to energize each crowd individually.

Embodying the Written Word

Jokes spring to life through believably delivered performances. Whether enthusiasm, emphatic line readings or character-driven inflections, commit fully to each word owning material authentically. Commitment translates scripts into kinetic experiences felt viscerally by all.

By regularly applying these tested principles, comedians cultivate finely tuned instincts for rhythm, pacing and delivery nuances. Over time, comedic timing becomes second nature propelling each performance to new engaging heights. With dedication, any comic can achieve mastery commanding crowds through the pulse of perfect delivery.

Connecting With Your Audience

Building genuine rapport with crowds lies at the heart of any strong performance. This section provides guidance on techniques for forging authentic bonds between comic and listener. From cultivating approachability through body language and style, to finely tuning crowd interactions, real relationships transform routine delivery into memorable shared experiences. With practice applying principles like active listening, charismatic presence and thoughtful questioning, comedians can organically engage listeners fully investing in experiences. Regular focus on connection building empowers full rooms of supporters energizing each show through laughter's communal spirit.

Projecting Approachability

A relaxed, open and unguarded body posture that utilizes natural eye contact combined with warm, inviting smiles is key to radiating genuine safety and comfort from the stage in order to attract similar positive energies from the audience. Through confident yet unhurried and unforced movements that are dynamically attuned to the material, cues, and crowd interaction, emanate a welcoming aura that encourages full participation from onlookers. Radiating complete ease and enjoyment in your own skin through candid physicality and facial expressions prompts audiences to let their guards down as well. This cultivated feel of friendly approachability draws in like-minded spirits and serves as a primed launching pad for rewarding comedic alchemy and interactive chemistry to readily unfold. With practice, autonomous signals of warmth, confidence and non-defensive fun prove catalysts for strong rapport building on stage and in the rooms.

Reading the Room

An expert comedian reads the energetic contours of the room with laser focus, actively tracking even the subtlest shifts in attentiveness across both individual jokes and full sets. Through intuitive attunement to the volume, duration and tonality of laughs, sighs or periods of silence, their delivery adapts fluidly, speeding up or slowing down, leaning into certain bits more heavily or lighter based on the feedback. This dynamic responsiveness breathes life into the material, matching and massaging the vibe fluctuations to ensure continued engagement from the audience. Rather than resting on predetermined structures, these adept performers spontaneously react to cues, fostering truly interactive performances that adapt uniquely to each crowd. The art of reading the room allows a deeper connection, as audiences feel heard, seen and reciprocally enjoyed through the comedian's nimble, empathetic adjustments that guide the energy of the collective experience comfortably upwards set after set.

Inviting Participation

Strong comedians realize the power of inclusive performance styles that strategically weave call-and-response bits, subtle callbacks to prior observations, and other playfully interactive moments throughout their sets. These inserts invite the warmest sense of communal camaraderie as audiences feel invested in creating bit characters, catchphrases or scenarios alongside the performer. Whether gleaning jokes from signs in the room or initiating lighthearted polls that build group rapport, techniques that yield spontaneous collaborations through improvisational pivots strengthen the bonds of creative co-authorship between stage and seats. Deeper involvement fosters stakes in shared successes that energize rooms collectively. Remembering audiences wish to feel part of something larger, the invitation to participate honors their dreams of belonging by spotlighting even marginal witty quips or natural wit from engagers, promoting goodwill that deepens investments in future shows.

Asking Thoughtful Questions

Gauging the Crowd Through Polite Inquiry

Comedians can effectively gauge a crowd's temperament and find relatable touchpoints by posing polite, thoughtful questions to audiences. Inquires aimed at open discussion or personal observation gently probe the contours of a group's character while signaling care, curiosity and willingness to understand diverse perspectives. The resulting shares of authentic views often unveil surprising unity that can dissipate dividing surface differences.

Transforming Strangers into Community

Furthermore, questions posed with lighthearted care can immediately dispel any sense of "othering" strangers may feel upon entering. This resets the energy to one of warmth, inclusion and newly formed intimate familiarity. As the comedian guides the discovery of common threads quietly linking all present, the very chemistry of a room transforms - changing mere spectators into invested communal bonds of compassionate dialogue. Curiosity fosters understanding while dispelling initial divisions, allowing any gathering of individuals to feel like earnestly bonded families.

Embodying Charisma

Comedians who master the art of commanding stage presence through vibrant facial expressions, animated body language and varied vocal tonality possess a rare charismatic gift. They devote themselves wholly to infusing performances with enthusiasm, fun and warm emotion. Every movement, vocal shift and gleam in their eye works synergistically to fuel audiences' imaginations and transport them to new comic realms. Their magnetizing personalities effortlessly draw kindred souls into communal bonds. Rooms filled with like-minded spirits eagerly latch onto these performers' every word and gesture, fully immersed and united in shared mirth. Such is the power of true comedic charisma to unite strangers as Brothers through nothing but joy, vivacity and love.

Sharing Vulnerabilities

Opening Through Humility

Comedians who expose their imperfect humanity by recounting past failures, mistakes, and laugh-lined weaknesses establish an immediate empathic bond with audiences. Sharing vulnerabilities humbles performers while reminding all that flaws and continued learning are shared experiences. When public figures embrace their imperfections, it invites others to lower guards and connect through shared failings.

Common Ground of Support

Revealing common weaknesses helps form communal bonds by uniting crowds in recognizing our shared humanity. Listeners often feel inspired by others who overcome hurdles through resilience and humor. Such honesty fosters an environment where audiences encourage ongoing growth, rather than punishment for past errors. Shared imperfection becomes the foundation for supportive relationships between performers and fans on their collective learning paths.

Relating to Lifestyles

Tailoring for Diversity

Skilled comedians tailor their material to respect different audiences by including subtle nods or outright calls-outs to varied lifestyle experiences. This welcoming approach fosters truly cohesive, judgement-free safe spaces where all feel represented and validated. Relatable content embracing diversities honors each person's journey by meeting them where they stand.

Strengthening Communal Ties

Representation is a gift which uplifts communities by strengthening shared bonds between performers and Listeners. Whether tapping into lived experiences of varied cultures, orientations, abilities or beliefs - embracing diverse perspectives promotes inclusion. Fanning these flames of understanding through laughter cultivates closer-knit ties as audiences beam seeing life's rich tapestry reflected onstage before them through humor.

Cultivating Insider Humor

Skilled comedians know that cultivating insider humor is key to cementing loyal fanbases. References to past show moments, in-jokes from previous routines, and callbacks to shared experiences work to bind extended "families" of devoted listeners across multiple performances. Ongoing stories and spotlighting attendee milestones foster warm recognitions that strengthen communal bonds, fueling repeat attendance and deepening stakeholders' investment in a comedian's success. This crafting of personalized inside jokes becomes far more than comedy - it is the cultivation of priceless memories and tightknit relationships that endure for years beyond any single show.

Valuing Individuals

Comedians who truly value their craft recognize that personal, meaningful engagement with each individual in the audience is key to cultivating lifelong fans. Simple yet impactful acts like learning and remembering names, following up with specific audience members after shows, or checking in on their lives in genuinely caring ways treats each attendee as the valued VIP they are. Taking the time to form small yet potent personal connections and remarks that display active remembrance of details about people's lives leaves audiences feeling truly seen and inspired. These tailored specific recollections, either on stage through materials or off stage through follow ups, resonate deeply and remind each listener of their inherent worth. Such personalized valuation sparks memories and goodwill that motivate lifetime loyalty, as patrons forever cherish the feeling of importance derived from a comedian who notices, appreciates and respects them as individuals.

Celebrating Successes

Applauding efforts and achievements together unifies through pride. Communal victories serve as memorable highlights felt collectively for years resonating feel-goods.

By placing focused emphasis on these principles nightly, comedians convert rooms of strangers into invested communities. Connection nourishes both comic and crowds alike through laughter's bonds transcending superficiality into invested relationships sustaining careers. Ultimately, commitment to genuine human rapport transforms performative art into humanity's shared celebration.

Exercises: Solo Visualization Exercises for Confident Performance; Pair Exercises for Practicing Delivery and Timing

Regular practice is essential to reinforcing learned techniques and strengthening comedic muscles memory over time. This section provides both solo and collaborative performance exercises to help comedians systematically improve skills like timing, delivery, stage presence and handling live audiences. Visualization exercises condition the mind for confident shows while pair workouts refine nuances receiving real-time feedback. Committed application of prompts cultivates autonomous abilities alongside invaluable insights from peer perspectives. Used consistently, these tried-and-true exercises effectively accelerate mastery of live comedy performance craft.

Solo Visualization Exercises

Mental Run-Throughs

Regularly visualizing the smooth performance of one's full material aids mental rehearsal like no other method. Performers can visualize each bit, transition, and crowd interaction from start to finish while mentally rehearsing sets in their entirety. This powerful solo imagery conditions the unconscious mind and physical muscle memory needed for success on stage. It also boosts confidence through the simulated experience of successful shows.

Delivery Drills

Alone time allows for focused physical practice of each routine while consciously emphasizing delivery through varying vocal tones, paces, facial expressions and gestures. Repetition embodies the full essence of each joke so it resides on the performer's comedic instincts. Internalizing the nuanced timing, tonality and physicality most conducive to landing each punchline trains the body perfectly for show time.

Pre-Show Visualization

Prior to stepping on stages, taking quiet moments to reinforce deep relaxation is paramount for confidence. Visualizing calm entrances, charming crowd scan work, and playfully interactive moments imagines an ideal stage presence and alleviates potential anxieties. These positive presets reset mental vibes, optimizing comedic flow state when curtains rise by conditioning the mind for joyful performance enjoyment rather than fearful "what if" scenarios.

Powerful Presence

Alone, stand tall with squared shoulders as you make confident eye contact with an imaginary packed audience before you. Through regular solo disposition rehearsals, own the invisible space with charmingly relaxed yet powerful body language. Embody how a natural stage persona would inhabit the room with ease. Envision charismatic facial expressions and gestures that Welcome each spectator warmly into the shared experience with you. These visualization techniques condition both physical muscle memory and mental self-assurance for commanding live performances.

Improvisation Imagery

Strengthen flexibility and quick-wittedness by often visualizing yourself smoothly rolling with hypothetical crowd retorts, tag suggestions, unexpected audience questions or other surprise scenario shifts during shows. Imagine seamlessly adjusting material angles or commencing lively impromptu conversations to keep the energy flowing high. Envision being a masterful problem-solver who welcomes unpredictable pivots with ease. Regularly rehearsing versatile improvisation imagery in this manner trains the mind and instincts for resilient stage presence, reaction times and witty social skills to effectively engage any crowd.

Pair Delivery Practice

Read-Aloud Trading

By exchanging fully written routines and performing each other's material live, comedic partners gain invaluable outside perspective and feedback. Receiving real-time comments on delivery flow, timing adherence and what lands best sharpens both parties' skills. These read-throughs allow subtle performance nuances to be caught that the author misses alone. Collaboration strengthens all.

Highlight Reel Showcases

Taking turns choosing each other's absolute strongest bits allows partners to truly analyze delivery nuances like emphasis, pacing and when to amp energy. They can pinpoint specifically what made certain moments remarkably funnier than others for deeper learning. Iterative fine-tuning through such collaborative breakdowns elevates overall material quality.

Line-By-Line Analysis:

Line-By-Line Analysis allows for in-depth delivery dissection. Performers take turns delivering single jokes, receiving focused feedback on subtle voice and physical optimizations. Partners identify precise breath or emphasis adjustments extending comedic effect. Repeating material with variations cultivates new perspectives on elevating impact. This rigorous iterative process of collaborative live experimentation and critique trains comedians to expertly craft impeccable delivery maximizing every line's hilarious potential.

Follow-The-Leader

Mirrored live practice fosters healthy competition and fun while cementing learned skills. One comedian traces through a delivery blueprint while the other copies techniques - whether distinct facial expressions, body motion or vocal cadences. This playful spontaneity reinforces the autonomous yet charismatic stage presence required to transport audiences.

Character Challenge:

The Character Challenge flexes improvisational acting skills. Comedians spontaneously embody roles and debate one another in character, practicing nuanced vocal and physical adaptations. Authentically inhabiting diverse personalities on the fly before an engaged partner cultivates deft delivery range. This spur of the moment persona interplay hones a comedian's nimble versatility to engage audiences with distinctively crafted dimensioned characters.

Mock Interactions

Roleplaying hypothetical crowd scenarios trains quick wit and flexibility and bolsters confidence in facing unknowns. Partners seamlessly handle unexpected disruptions, ensuing dialogues and complex call-and-response exchanges together in the moment. Such extemporaneous collaboration develops authentic mastery of socially skilled performance versatility.

The Art of Pausing Practice:

The Art of Pausing Practice is a crucial exercise for comedians. Trading off material, partners methodically insert, remove or alter minute, calculated pauses and rests. Through live experimentation, they naturally progress comedic tension and discover optimal timing. Various inflectional hesitations are tested to find which subtly elevate specific punchlines or story climaxes. Iterative collaboration continually refines pausing technique. Mastery of this nuanced comedic tool emerges as they intuitively learn where suspenseful pauses maximize laughs.

These mental and collaborative drills systematically condition comedians' physical instincts reinforcing skills like second nature. Committed application cultivates autonomous abilities while cultivating invaluable peer perspectives accelerating mastery.

Solo Exercises

Shadow Performance

Recording solo performances for close self-analysis is extremely valuable. Play back scrutinizing vocal nuances, facial expressions, gestures and physical behaviors - making subtle notes on refinements that strengthen presence and resonate delivery. Repeated review trains an eye for optimizing captivating stage composition from all vantage points.

Stage Movement Practice

Choreographing purposeful movement patterns that complement certain jokes or bits allows natural incorporation on stage. Solo run-throughs with planned motions integrated into material builds muscle memory. Flowing through routines while envisioning the visual experience of an audience cements spatial ownership and interaction that engages captivated spectators.

Props Delivery Drills

Incorporating random props from one's surroundings into solo routine recitations gets comfortable physically handling objects and seamlessly incorporating non-verbal components. Play builds dexterity and quick-wittedness and reveals opportunities to elevate material with visual aids. Iterative experimentation cultivates mastery of an effortless prop-inclusive performance style.

Character Journaling

Developing background histories, motivations, quirks, and distinctive voices of characters through first-person journal writing exercises strengthens commitment to dimensionality on stage. Getting inside imagined personalities' minds informs empathetic role inhabitation and nuanced performance qualities that transport audiences believably into crafted worlds.

Pair Exercises

Blind Line Delivery

Blind Line Delivery flexes improvisational skills through surprise. Partners pass slips of random punchlines without context. Delivering with varying tones, timings and physicality trains quick adaptation. Gauging real-time feedback on divergent delivery experimentation fosters versatile presence.

Feed Line Games

Feed Line Games cultivate whip-smart reactiveness under pressure. Taking turns providing partial lines, partners must fill punchlines on the spot. Playful interactivity exercises improvised wit while bolstering bonding over collaborative laughter. Fluid repartee nurtures magnetic stage dynamics.

Scenario Swaps

Scenario Swaps strengthen dexterous adaptation by trading set contexts. Fluidly performing each other's routines in unexpected environments displays resilient comedic flexibility. Imaginative "what if" scenarios uncover nuances elevating any material's relatability.

Car Rides

Car Rides provide unique presence practice. Delivering sets while driving means projecting engagement without visual cues. Smooth impromptu transitions amid distractions fortifies stage command in any conditions. Autonomous road show training strengthens resilient performance skills.

Stand-Up Karaoke

Stand-Up Karaoke synchronizes finely-honed delivery muscles. Silently mouthing routines tests locked-in comedic timing correspondence. Identifying discrepancies improves autonomous pacing mastery for reliably landing perfect rhythm and pacing.

Heckler Roleplays

Heckler Roleplays prepare for unpredictable surprises. Taking turns instigating disruptions, partners must calibrate improv to pacify through charming repartee. Real-time scenarios develop sociable rapid-fire wit bolstering crowd-work confidence.

These additional brainstorming challenges complement the core exercises by pushing comedians' creative problem-solving and flexibility under simulated performance conditions for well-rounded mastery.

CHAPTER 4

HANDLING HECKLERS
LIKE PRO

While every comedian dreams of a perfectly engaged crowd enjoying their routine, the reality is that occasionally someone will interrupt or try to disrupt the flow of a performance. These unwieldy audience members, known as hecklers, can throw off even the most experienced comics if not handled properly. In this chapter, readers will learn proven techniques for keeping composure when faced with an unruly listener and regaining control of the crowd.

Dealing with a heckler requires maintaining presence of mind under pressure so the performance does not spiral off course. A skilled comedian will be able to think on their feet and turn even disruptive comments back around to further entertain the rest of the room. The key is not letting a single rude voice overshadow the overall experience for everyone else. With the right strategies in their arsenal, any comic can navigate unplanned interruptions and come out on top with the crowd still firmly in the palm of their hands.

This chapter will outline both verbal and nonverbal methods for effectively silencing would-be hecklers while keeping momentum. Topics will include establishing dominance through posture and eye contact, crafting improvised comebacks, getting the crowd on your side, and bringing disruptors into the act in a way that reinforces you are in control of the stage. Mastering these techniques empowers comedians to hit any live situation with confidence and the ability to roll with unexpected punches.

Understanding Heckler Psychology

To effectively handle disruptions during live shows, it is important for comedians to gain insight into the motivations behind troublesome audience behaviors. This section aims to demystify the psychology of hecklers by exploring common types and their triggers. Understanding what provokes interruptions enables preemption through subtle crowd monitoring and subsequent redirection tactics. With guidance on identifying intentions behind unwelcome outbursts and adjusting responses accordingly, performers can more confidently roll with unpredictable moments harnessing them for the room's collective enjoyment. Mastering this topic empowers comedians to navigate disturbances while retaining full control and momentum.

The Attention Seeker

Some hecklers seek any kind of attention, positive or negative. By observing signs like excited grins or fidgeting that show pent-up energy, their disruption can be redirected constructively. A few quick remarks that acknowledge their desire for attention while humorously exaggerating their comments can shift focus back to the audience, maintaining the comedic flow. It's crucial to keep responses brief to prevent the heckler from dominating the event for too long and disrupting the performance schedule.

The Loudmouth Bully

Often, loud confidence often comes from hiding deep-seated insecurities, using aggressive comments to seek attention as a temporary relief. Maintaining a relaxed posture, friendly eye contact, and a casual tone can reduce the appeal of provoking reactions. Friendly, self-deprecating jokes can acknowledge and deflate pretentious behavior with laughter, soothing tensions and deflating egos without escalating conflict or feeding dominance-seeking behavior unnecessarily.

The Contrarian Complainer

People inclined toward argument often seek validation of their views, speaking up mainly to counter arguments. Redirecting attention with humor can turn dissatisfaction into laughter, bringing people together constructively. Asking respectful questions that invite their perspective can reduce hostility and foster camaraderie, guiding discussions toward positive directions and steering away from divisive viewpoints.

The Drunk Instigator

When alcohol loosens inhibitions and triggers interruptions, responding with light-hearted humor can redirect attention back to the enjoyment of the group. By playfully exaggerating the effects of alcohol through comedy, it acknowledges the situation while diffusing tensions and fostering communal laughter. This approach not only handles disruptions caused by impaired judgment but also enhances the group's sense of camaraderie and collective enjoyment. It ensures that everyone can continue to share in the jovial atmosphere without distractions.

The Bored Observer

When complacency leads to restlessness in some individuals, often due to moments of boredom or overstimulation wearing off, it's important to re-engage them in a positive manner. This can be achieved by acknowledging their observations or responding to impromptu questions with enthusiasm and inclusivity. For example, if someone in the audience seems disengaged or bored during a presentation or event, the speaker could playfully draw attention to them in a positive way.

By doing so, they not only recognize the individual's presence but also involve them in the collective enjoyment. This approach can effectively lift the energy of the entire group by transforming potential moments of restlessness into opportunities for shared amusement and camaraderie. It highlights the power of humor and inclusivity in maintaining a lively and engaging atmosphere, countering any temporary lapses in attention or interest with renewed enthusiasm.

The Covert Smirker

Subtly expressed judgments through smirks or eyerolls often provoke defensive reactions, but this friction can be diplomatically defused by using warm self-deprecation. By humorously acknowledging one's own flaws or mistakes before others have a chance to react critically, tension can be preemptively diffused. For instance, if someone notices others reacting with skepticism or amusement, they might disarm the situation by joking about their own quirks or past blunders. This approach not only shows self-awareness but also invites others to join in shared laughter, turning potential misunderstandings into moments of mutual understanding and camaraderie. It highlights the power of humor in bridging gaps and fostering a more relaxed and inclusive atmosphere, where everyone feels comfortable and connected despite differences.

The Emotional Wound-Picker

Unresolved past traumas can sometimes lead to present aggression, especially when triggered by perceived or imagined offenses. However, handling interruptions with empathy and compassion can elevate everyone's mood. By patiently and empathetically addressing hecklers who may be acting out of their own unresolved pain, it becomes possible to redirect their energy toward shared laughter and camaraderie. This approach aims to foster a sense of fellowship rather than aggravate discord.

By guiding disruptive energies into positive and healing interactions, we can prevent further escalation of hostilities. Together in a positive atmosphere, even the most profound pains can find comfort and healing through mutual understanding and support.

The Cynical Critic

When chronic dissatisfaction seeks to disrupt harmony by souring the atmosphere, addressing this challenge with an inclusive and hopeful outlook can restore unity through laughter. Speaking to both the audience and critics with passionate yet balanced reminders of our shared humanity can subtly transform negativity into warmth through collective bonding. Even the coldest expressions of toxicity can be thawed by goodwill and communal empathy, guided by a shared focus on our common interests and aspirations.

By understanding motivations behind disruptions and responding appropriately, we can neutralize tensions for the benefit of all involved. Enduring through unpredictable moments not only builds resilience but also rewards audiences with a sense of shared experience and connection. Ultimately, comedy succeeds in uniting diverse individuals joyfully into a cohesive community, celebrating our shared humanity and the power of humor to uplift spirits and foster understanding.

Strategies For Dealing with Hecklers

Understanding the Psychology of Hecklers

Hecklers are an unfortunate reality in the world of stand-up comedy. To effectively deal with them, it's crucial to understand their motivations. Recent studies in performance psychology have shed light on why some audience members feel compelled to disrupt shows.

Dr. Sophie Richards, a renowned psychologist specializing in performer-audience dynamics, explains, "Hecklers often act out of a desire for attention or a misguided attempt to participate in the show. In some cases, it's a manifestation of insecurity or a need to assert dominance in a public setting."

Understanding these motivations can help comedians approach hecklers with empathy while maintaining control. For instance, famous comedian Dave Chappelle once dealt with a persistent heckler by saying, "I bet you're the kind of guy who thinks he's funny at parties, but everyone's just too polite to tell you to shut up." This response not only silenced the heckler but also demonstrated an understanding of the psychology behind the interruption.

It's also important to recognize that not all hecklers are malicious. Sometimes, audience members interject out of enthusiasm or a misguided attempt to contribute to the show. In 2023, rising star comedian Sarah Chen shared her experience: "I had a guy shout out punchlines before I could finish my setups. It was annoying, but I realized he was just overly excited about the show. I had to find a way to channel that energy without shutting him down completely."

By understanding the various motivations behind heckling, comedians can tailor their responses more effectively, turning potential show-ruining moments into opportunities for even bigger laughs.

Preventive Measures: Setting the Right Tone

The best way to deal with hecklers is to prevent them from speaking up in the first place. This starts with setting the right tone from the moment you step on stage. Many successful comedians have developed strategies to establish their authority and create an atmosphere that discourages interruptions.

Veteran comedian and coach Terry Sullivan advises, "Your opening minutes are crucial. You need to project confidence and control from the get-go. If you seem unsure or timid, it's like blood in the water for potential hecklers."

One effective technique is to address the audience directly about heckling at the beginning of your set. In 2024, rising star comic Alex Rodriguez gained viral attention for his unique approach: "Before I start, let's make a deal. I won't come to your job and knock the mop out of your hands, so don't come to mine and shout out random bullshit. Deal? Great!"

This approach not only sets clear expectations but also gets a laugh, starting the show on a positive note. It's important, however, to tailor this approach to your personal style and the venue. What works in a rowdy club might not be appropriate for a corporate gig.

Another preventive measure is to engage with the audience early in your set, but on your terms. Ask rhetorical questions or use call-and-response techniques that give the audience a controlled way to participate. This can satisfy the urge some people have to be part of the show without opening the door to disruptive behavior.

Comedian Lisa Wong shares her strategy: "I like to do a quick audience check-in at the start. I'll ask things like 'Who's here on a date?' or 'Who's celebrating something tonight?' It gives people a chance to shout out and feel involved, but I'm the one controlling the interaction."

By setting the right tone and giving the audience appropriate outlets for participation, you can significantly reduce the likelihood of disruptive heckling during your set.

Quick-Witted Comebacks: The Art of the Rapid Response

When prevention fails and a heckler does pipe up, having a arsenal of quick-witted comebacks can be a comedian's best defense. The key is to respond rapidly and decisively, shutting down the interruption before it can derail your set.

Legendary comic Patton Oswalt emphasizes the importance of speed: "You've got to be faster than the heckler. If you hesitate, you've lost the room. Your comeback needs to be instant and devastating."

One effective technique is to have a set of all-purpose responses ready to go. These should be adaptable to various situations and deliverable without much thought. For example, comedian Sarah Silverman is known for her go-to line: "I'm sorry, did the middle of my show interrupt the beginning of your conversation?"

However, relying solely on pre-prepared lines can come across as inauthentic or robotic. The real art lies in crafting responses that are both quick and tailored to the specific situation. This requires practice and the ability to think on your feet.

In 2023, during a live-streamed performance, comedian Trevor Noah demonstrated this skill brilliantly. When a heckler shouted, "You're not funny!" Noah instantly replied, "Sir, I think you're at the wrong show. The mirror store is next door." This response not only silenced the heckler but also earned a huge laugh from the audience, seamlessly integrating the interruption into his act.

Another approach is to use the heckler's own words against them. Comic veteran Joan Rivers was a master of this technique. When a heckler once shouted, "You're fat!" she immediately shot back, "No, you're fat. See? I can be a bad comedian too."

The key to mastering quick-witted comebacks is practice. Many comedians incorporate heckling scenarios into their rehearsals, having friends shout random interruptions to help them develop their rapid response skills. This preparation can make the difference between a show-stopping heckler and a minor speed bump in your set.

Crowd Control: Enlisting the Audience's Support

One of the most powerful tools in dealing with hecklers is the rest of the audience. Most people come to a comedy show to enjoy the performance, not to hear random shouts from other attendees. Skilled comedians know how to enlist the crowd's support in shutting down disruptive behavior.

Comedy club owner and former stand-up comic Maria Sanchez explains, "When you effectively handle a heckler, you're not just defending yourself, you're championing the entire audience's right to enjoy the show they paid for."

One technique is to directly appeal to the audience's sense of fairness. In a 2024 performance, comedian John Mulaney dealt with a persistent heckler by saying, "Okay, let's take a vote. Who wants to hear more from this guy, and who wants to hear the show they actually paid for?" The resulting chorus of boos effectively silenced the heckler without Mulaney having to engage in a one-on-one confrontation.

Another approach is to use the heckler's interruption as a springboard for crowd interaction. Comedian Tig Notaro demonstrated this brilliantly during a 2023 show in Chicago. When a drunk audience member kept shouting nonsensical comments, Notaro turned to the rest of the crowd and said, "I think we just found our translator for the evening. Sir, can you please interpret everything I say for the rest of the show?" This not only diffused the situation but turned the heckler into an unwitting part of the act, much to the audience's delight.

It's important, however, to read the room correctly. In some cases, directly confronting a heckler can create tension that makes the audience uncomfortable. Comedian and author Steve Hofstetter advises, "If you sense that the audience is on edge, sometimes it's better to briefly acknowledge the heckler and move on. You can say something like, 'Thank you for your contribution, sir. Now, as I was saying before I was so rudely interrupted by the person who apparently thought this was a sing-along...'"

By skillfully managing these situations, you not only shut down the heckler but also strengthen your connection with the rest of the audience, often resulting in a more engaged and appreciative crowd for the remainder of your set.

De-escalation Techniques: Keeping Cool Under Pressure

While quick comebacks and audience support are valuable tools, sometimes the best approach to dealing with hecklers is de-escalation. This is particularly important when facing aggressive or intoxicated individuals who might not respond well to direct confrontation.

Comedian and conflict resolution expert Dr. Laura Martinez emphasizes the importance of staying calm: "Your goal is to diffuse the situation, not win an argument. If you match a heckler's aggression, you risk losing control of the room and potentially escalating the situation to a dangerous level."

One effective de-escalation technique is to use self-deprecating humor. By making yourself the target of the joke, you can often disarm a hostile heckler. For example, when faced with a particularly aggressive heckler in 2023, comedian Jim Gaffigan responded, "Sir, I understand your anger. I'd be mad too if I paid to see me." This unexpected response not only got a laugh but also seemed to confuse and calm the heckler.

Another approach is to acknowledge the heckler's point, even if you disagree with it. This can help the heckler feel heard and reduce their need to continue interrupting. During a 2024 performance, comedian Wanda Sykes demonstrated this technique when a heckler shouted that her joke about politics was biased. Sykes responded, "You know what? You're right. I am biased. I'm biased towards things that are funny. Now, can I get back to being biased, or do you have more notes for me?"

It's also important to know when to involve venue security. If a heckler becomes too disruptive or shows signs of potential violence, it's better to let professionals handle the situation. Comedian Chris Rock advises, "Know your limits. If you feel threatened or if the heckler is ruining the show for everyone, it's okay to ask for help. Your safety and the audience's enjoyment should always come first."

By mastering these de-escalation techniques, comedians can maintain control of difficult situations without resorting to confrontational tactics that might backfire.

Learning and Adapting: Post-Heckler Analysis

Dealing with hecklers is as much about learning from past experiences as it is about in-the-moment reactions. Successful comedians often treat heckler encounters as opportunities for growth and improvement.

Comedy coach and former club owner Rachel Lee suggests, "After every show, especially ones where you've had to deal with hecklers, take some time to reflect on what happened. What worked? What didn't? How could you have handled it better?"

Many comedians keep a "heckler journal" where they record their experiences and brainstorm better responses for future encounters. For instance, comedian Aziz Ansari shared in a 2024 interview that he reviews his heckler interactions regularly: "I'll write down exactly what the heckler said and how I responded. Then I'll spend some time coming up with five or six alternative comebacks. It's like building a muscle – the more you practice, the better you get."

It's also valuable to seek feedback from other comedians or even trusted audience members. They might offer perspectives or insights you missed in the heat of the moment. Veteran comic Dave Attell is known for his willingness to mentor younger comedians in this area: "I always tell new comics to find me after a show if they had a rough time with a heckler. Sometimes an outside perspective can help you see solutions you might have missed."

Another important aspect of post-heckler analysis is recognizing patterns. Are you consistently dealing with hecklers during certain types of jokes or at particular points in your set? This information can help you adjust your material or delivery to minimize future interruptions.

Lastly, it's crucial to remember that even the most skilled comedians occasionally struggle with hecklers. Don't be too hard on yourself if an interaction doesn't go as smoothly as you'd like. Each experience is an opportunity to learn and improve your craft.

Turning Heckling Situations Into Opportunities

The Art of Improvisation: Thinking on Your Feet

One of the most valuable skills a comedian can develop when dealing with hecklers is the ability to improvise. Turning a potentially disruptive situation into comedy gold requires quick thinking and adaptability. This skill not only helps in handling hecklers but can also elevate your overall performance.

Renowned improvisation coach and comedian Sarah Thompson explains, "Improvisation is about being present in the moment and reacting authentically to what's happening around you. When a heckler interrupts, it's an opportunity to create something unique and spontaneous."

A prime example of this skill in action occurred during a 2023 performance by John Mulaney. When a heckler shouted, "You're not as funny as you think you are!" Mulaney immediately responded, "Well, sir, I'm afraid you've grossly overestimated how funny I think I am." This quick-witted response not only diffused the situation but also got a huge laugh from the audience, turning a potential setback into a highlight of the show.

To develop this skill, many comedians incorporate improvisation exercises into their practice routines. One popular technique is the "Yes, and..." approach, where you accept what's been said and build upon it. Comedian Tina Fey, known for her improv background, often uses this technique when dealing with hecklers. In a 2024 show, when an audience member shouted out a random word, Fey seamlessly incorporated it into her routine, saying, "Yes, and speaking of 'platypus,' let me tell you about my last dating experience..."

Another key aspect of improvisation is listening actively. Instead of just waiting for your turn to speak or thinking about your prepared material, really hear what the heckler is saying. This can provide fodder for an even funnier response. Stand-up veteran Dave Chappelle is a master of this technique. During a 2023 performance, when a heckler made a nonsensical comment about elephants, Chappelle paused, then launched into an impromptu bit about "elephant hecklers" that had the audience in stitches.

Remember, the goal of improvisation in these situations is not just to shut down the heckler, but to create a memorable moment that enhances your performance. As improv guru Del Close famously said, "Follow the fear." Don't be afraid to take risks and go to unexpected places with your responses. The audience will appreciate your quick wit and ability to handle the unexpected.

Crowd Work: Engaging the Audience

Crowd work, the art of interacting directly with audience members, can be a powerful tool for turning heckling situations into opportunities. By engaging with the crowd, you can often diffuse tension, create unique moments, and even generate new material on the spot.

Veteran comedian and crowd work expert Jeff Ross emphasizes the importance of this skill: "Crowd work isn't just about dealing with hecklers. It's about making every show unique and building a connection with your audience. When you're good at crowd work, even a heckler becomes just another audience member to play with."

One effective technique is to use the heckler as a springboard for engaging with other audience members. For example, in a 2024 performance, Ali Wong masterfully handled a drunk heckler by turning to the people sitting near him and asking, "Is this your friend? Who brought this guy? I hope you got a group discount, because he's clearly here to perform his own show." This not only shut down the heckler but also created a fun interaction with the rest of the audience.

Another approach is to incorporate the heckler's comments into your prepared material. Comedian Patton Oswalt demonstrated this brilliantly during a 2023 show. When a heckler interrupted his bit about fast food, Oswalt smoothly transitioned, saying, "Speaking of things that leave a bad taste in your mouth, let's talk about this guy's contribution to the show." He then wove the heckler's comment into his routine, creating a unique and hilarious moment.

It's important to note that effective crowd work requires reading the room and understanding the dynamics of your audience. Comedy club owner and former stand-up Maria Sanchez advises, "Pay attention to the energy in the room. If the audience seems uncomfortable with direct confrontation, use softer crowd work techniques. Ask questions, make observations about the venue or the city you're in. This can help reset the energy without putting anyone on the spot."

Some comedians even incorporate planned "heckler" moments into their shows to practice their crowd work skills. In 2024, upcoming comedian Jake Chen made waves with his "Plant a Heckler" tour, where he had a friend in each audience start heckling at a specific point in the show. This allowed Chen to showcase his crowd work skills while also creating a unique experience for the audience.

Remember, the goal of crowd work in these situations is to maintain control of the room while creating an inclusive and entertaining atmosphere. As comedy legend Don Rickles once said, "I don't care if you laugh at me, but I want you to laugh with me."

Reframing the Narrative: Turning Negatives into Positives

One of the most powerful techniques for turning heckling situations into opportunities is the ability to reframe the narrative. This involves taking a potentially negative situation and spinning it into something positive, often to comedic effect.

Dr. Lisa Martinez, a psychologist specializing in performance anxiety, explains, "Reframing is a cognitive technique that can help comedians maintain their composure and even thrive under pressure. By changing your perspective on the situation, you can transform a threat into an opportunity."

A classic example of this technique in action comes from comedian Jimmy Carr. Known for his sharp comebacks, Carr once dealt with a heckler who shouted, "Tell us a joke!" Instead of getting defensive, Carr reframed the situation, responding, "I've been doing that for the past hour. I know the club's got shitty lighting, but surely you noticed you were at a comedy show?" This response not only shut down the heckler but also got a big laugh from the audience.

Reframing can also involve turning the heckler's words back on them in an unexpected way. In a 2023 performance, rising star comedian Sarah Chen demonstrated this brilliantly. When a heckler shouted, "You suck!", Chen paused, then said, "Wow, I didn't realize my ex was in the audience tonight. How are you, Brad? Still living in your mom's basement?" By reframing the heckler's insult as a comment from an ex-partner, Chen created a humorous scenario that the audience could engage with.

Another effective reframing technique is to use self-deprecating humor. By making yourself the target of the joke, you can often disarm a heckler and win the audience's sympathy. Comedian Kumail Nanjiani employed this strategy during a 2024 show when a heckler criticized his accent. Nanjiani responded, "I know, right? I've been trying to get rid of this American accent for years, but it just won't go away." This unexpected twist on the heckler's racist comment not only got a laugh but also made the heckler look foolish.

It's important to note that effective reframing requires quick thinking and a willingness to be vulnerable. Comedy coach Terry Sullivan advises, "Don't be afraid to admit when a heckler has gotten under your skin. Sometimes, acknowledging the awkwardness of the situation can be the best way to move past it."

By mastering the art of reframing, comedians can turn potentially show-stopping interruptions into some of the most memorable and entertaining moments of their performances.

Creating Callbacks: Weaving Hecklers into Your Set

One of the most sophisticated ways to turn a heckling situation into an opportunity is by creating callbacks to the incident throughout your set. This technique not only showcases your quick wit but also demonstrates your ability to craft cohesive, engaging performances on the fly.

Veteran comedian and writing coach Sarah Silverman explains, "A good callback can turn a random heckle into a running joke that enhances your entire set. It shows the audience that you're in control and can weave even unexpected elements into your performance."

For example, during a 2023 performance, comedian John Mulaney dealt with a heckler who shouted out "Banana!" at a random moment. Instead of just shutting down the heckler, Mulaney incorporated the word "banana" into several subsequent jokes, each time acknowledging the original heckler with a nod. By the end of the show, "banana" had become an inside joke between Mulaney and the audience, creating a unique, shared experience.

Creating effective callbacks requires a balance of spontaneity and structure. Comedy writer Jake Johnson advises, "When you get a good response to a heckler interaction, make a mental note. Think about how you can reference it later in your set, but in a way that feels natural, not forced."

Some comedians even prepare flexible spots in their sets where they can insert callbacks to earlier interactions. In 2024, rising star Alex Rodriguez gained attention for his "Heckler's Choice" tour, where he left deliberate gaps in his set to incorporate material generated from audience interactions.

It's important to note that not every heckler interaction warrants a callback. Comedy club owner Maria Sanchez cautions, "Be selective.

Only call back to moments that genuinely resonated with the audience. If you try to force a callback to a flat interaction, you risk losing the crowd's engagement."

When done well, callbacks can create a sense of continuity and shared experience that elevates your entire performance. As legendary comedian Richard Pryor once said, "The best comedy comes from pain." By transforming the "pain" of a heckler into a source of ongoing humor, you demonstrate true mastery of your craft.

Professional Development: Learning from Heckler Interactions

While dealing with hecklers in the moment is crucial, equally important is the ability to learn and grow from these experiences. Successful comedians view heckler interactions not just as challenges to overcome, but as opportunities for professional development.

Comedy coach and former club owner Rachel Lee emphasizes the importance of reflection: "After every show, especially ones where you've had to deal with hecklers, take some time to analyze what happened. What worked? What didn't? How could you have handled it better? This kind of self-reflection is key to improving your craft."

Many comedians keep detailed journals of their heckler interactions, using them as a resource for developing new material and improving their crowd work skills. For instance, in his 2024 memoir "Laugh Lines and Battle Scars," comedian Aziz Ansari revealed that he reviews his heckler encounters weekly, brainstorming alternative responses and incorporating the best ones into future sets.

Peer review can also be a valuable tool for learning from heckler interactions. Comedy clubs like The Comedy Cellar in New York have started hosting "Heckler Workshops," where comedians can share their experiences and get feedback from their peers. Veteran comic Dave Attell, a regular participant, notes, "Sometimes it takes an outside perspective to see a brilliant comeback you missed in the heat of the moment."

Some comedians are even incorporating simulated heckling into their rehearsal processes. In 2023, rising star Sarah Chen made waves with her "Heckle Me" app, which plays random heckler comments during practice sessions, allowing comedians to hone their response skills in a low-pressure environment.

It's also important to recognize that not all heckler interactions will go smoothly, and that's okay. As comedy legend Joan Rivers once said, "In comedy, there are no mistakes, only moments of opportunity." Even a poorly handled heckler can provide valuable lessons for future performances.

Maintaining Control of The Stage

Establishing Authority from the Start

The moment a comedian steps on stage, the battle for control begins. Establishing authority quickly and effectively is crucial for maintaining control throughout the performance, especially when faced with potential disruptions like hecklers.

Veteran comedian and comedy coach Terry Sullivan emphasizes the importance of these first moments: "Your opening seconds on stage set the tone for the entire show. If you appear hesitant or unsure, it's like blood in the water for hecklers and other disruptive elements."

One effective technique for establishing authority is to use confident body language from the moment you're introduced. In 2023, rising star comedian Alex Rodriguez gained attention for his distinctive stage entrance. He would stride purposefully to the microphone, take a moment to survey the audience with a slight smile, and then launch into his set without preamble. This simple but powerful approach immediately communicated that he was in charge of the room.

Your opening lines are also crucial for establishing authority. Many successful comedians use what's known as a "snap" joke - a quick, punchy line delivered immediately after taking the stage. For instance, in her 2024 Netflix special, Sarah Silverman opened with: "Thank you! It's great to be here in [City Name]. I just flew in, and boy, are my arms tired of people using that joke." This immediate laugh not only warmed up the audience but also demonstrated Silverman's quick wit and control of the room.

Some comedians choose to directly address potential disruptions in their opening remarks. In a 2023 performance, Dave Chappelle began his set by saying, "Before we start, let's set some ground rules. I'm going to tell jokes, and you're going to laugh. If you feel the need to shout something out, remember - I have the microphone, and I'm funnier than you." This approach, delivered with Chappelle's characteristic dry humor, clearly established his authority while also getting a laugh.

It's also important to be aware of your physical presence on stage. Comedy movement coach Lisa Chen advises, "Own your space. Move purposefully, use the entire stage, and don't be afraid to take up room. Physical confidence translates to perceived authority."

Remember, establishing authority doesn't mean being aggressive or confrontational. As comedy legend Jerry Seinfeld once said, "The audience wants to like you. Your job is to give them permission to do so." By projecting confidence and control from the start, you create an environment where the audience feels comfortable and ready to laugh.

Mastering Stage Presence and Energy Control

Once you've established your initial authority, maintaining control of the stage requires consistent, strong stage presence and the ability to manage your energy throughout the performance. This is particularly crucial when faced with potential disruptions or a tough crowd.

Renowned performance coach Dr. Maria Sanchez explains, "Stage presence is about more than just being seen - it's about being felt. A comedian with great stage presence can hold an audience's attention even during moments of silence."

One key aspect of stage presence is maintaining eye contact with the audience. In his 2024 masterclass on comedy, Chris Rock revealed his technique: "I try to make eye contact with every section of the audience at least once during my set. It creates a connection and keeps people engaged, making them less likely to disrupt the show."

Energy control is equally important. Comedy veteran Wanda Sykes is known for her ability to modulate her energy to match and then guide the audience's mood. During a 2023 performance in Chicago, Sykes faced a subdued crowd. Instead of trying to force high energy, she lowered her own energy slightly and gradually built it up over the course of her set, bringing the audience along with her.

Voice modulation is another powerful tool for maintaining control. Vocal coach and former stand-up Jake Chen advises, "Vary your volume, pace, and tone. A well-timed pause or a sudden shift in volume can recapture a wandering audience's attention."

Physical movement on stage also plays a crucial role. In his 2024 tour, John Mulaney demonstrated masterful use of stage movement, using deliberate walks, gestures, and even dance moves to punctuate his jokes and keep the audience engaged. However, it's important to ensure that movement is purposeful. As comedy legend Steve Martin once said, "Be so good they can't ignore you."

Managing your own energy and emotions is crucial, especially when faced with a tough crowd or hecklers. In a 2023 interview, Ali Wong shared her technique: "I visualize myself as a conductor and the audience as my orchestra. Even if some instruments are out of tune, my job is to keep the overall performance on track."

Remember, maintaining control isn't about dominating the audience, but about guiding their experience. As George Carlin famously said, "I'm not up here to make you think I'm funny. I'm up here to make you think."

Crafting a Bulletproof Set Structure

A well-structured set is one of the most powerful tools a comedian has for maintaining control of the stage. A strong structure provides a framework that can help you stay on track even when faced with disruptions or unexpected audience reactions.

Comedy writer and structure expert Sarah Thompson explains, "Think of your set structure as a safety net. When everything's going well, the audience doesn't notice it. But when things get shaky, it's what keeps you from falling."

One popular structuring technique is the "callback" - referencing earlier jokes later in the set. In his 2023 Netflix special, Aziz Ansari demonstrated masterful use of callbacks, weaving references to earlier jokes throughout his set. This not only created a sense of cohesion but also gave him reliable laugh points to fall back on if a new joke didn't land as well as expected.

Another effective structuring technique is the "build" - starting with smaller jokes and gradually working up to bigger punchlines. In her 2024 tour, Hannah Gadsby used this technique to tackle increasingly complex and controversial topics, building audience trust with lighter material before delving into heavier subjects.

Many comedians also use a technique called "threading" - connecting seemingly unrelated jokes with a common theme. Dave Chappelle is a master of this technique. In his 2023 special, he wove together jokes about politics, race, and personal anecdotes, all connected by the theme of misunderstanding. This gave his act a sense of purpose and direction that helped maintain audience engagement.

It's also important to have flexibility within your structure. Comedy club owner Terry Sullivan advises, "Have a few 'floating' jokes that can be inserted at different points in your set. This allows you to adapt to the audience's energy without losing your overall structure."

Some comedians even incorporate planned "spontaneous" moments into their sets. In his 2024 tour, John Mulaney included a segment where he would "randomly" select an audience member to help with a bit. While the selection was pre-planned, it gave the illusion of spontaneity and helped keep the audience engaged.

Remember, the goal of structure isn't to make your set rigid, but to provide a framework that supports your performance. As George Carlin once said, "I'm not afraid to go off on tangents, but I always know how to get back to the main road."

Exercises: Solo Role-Playing Scenarios with Imaginary Hecklers; Pair Exercises for Practicing Responses to Heckling

While experience conquers most through authentic stage-time, intentional skill-strengthening between shows yields dividends. This section presents effective solo and partnered exercises optimizing disruption handling preparation. Solo role-playing imaginary hecklers aids improvisation muscle memory under practice duress. Partnered exchanges fine-tune nuanced techniques through collaborative simulations. Regular practice embeds instinctive abilities ensuring even adversity augments rather than hinders performances. Committing to ongoing growth nurtures abilities magnifying jokes while minimizing potential jitters. With guidance on maximizing preparatory practices, comedians emerge equipped and eager to rise above all by lifting others humorously.

Mirror Monologue

Setup:

Stand in front of a mirror with a microphone or a microphone-like object.

Exercise:

- Begin performing your stand-up routine as you normally would.
- At random intervals, interrupt yourself with heckler comments.
- Respond to these imaginary heckles out loud, maintaining eye contact with yourself in the mirror.
- Practice different types of responses: quick comebacks, crowd engagement, de-escalation techniques, etc.
- Aim for 10-15 minutes of continuous practice.

This exercise helps you practice maintaining composure, eye contact, and stage presence while dealing with hecklers. It also allows you to see your facial expressions and body language as you respond.

Recording Roulette

Setup:

Record a series of potential heckles on your phone or computer. Include a variety of comments, from mild interruptions to more aggressive heckling.

Exercise:

- Start performing your routine.
- Play the recorded heckles at random intervals.
- Respond to each heckle as it comes, trying to seamlessly incorporate your responses into your set.
- Continue your routine after each response, maintaining flow and energy.
- Practice for 20-30 minutes.

This exercise simulates the unpredictability of live heckling and helps you practice transitioning smoothly between your prepared material and heckler responses.

Scenario Simulation

Setup:

Write down 5-10 specific heckling scenarios on individual cards. These could include drunk hecklers, aggressive hecklers, audience members talking among themselves, etc.

Exercise:

- Randomly select a scenario card.
- Perform your routine, imagining the specific heckling situation described on the card.
- Practice appropriate responses and techniques for that particular scenario.
- After 5-10 minutes, switch to another randomly selected scenario.
- Continue for 30-45 minutes, covering various scenarios.

This exercise helps you prepare for a wide range of potential heckling situations, allowing you to develop specific strategies for different types of hecklers.

Pair Exercises for Practicing Responses to Heckling

Rapid-Fire Comeback Challenge

Setup: Two comedians face each other, one acting as the performer and the other as the heckler.

Exercise:

- The "performer" begins their routine.
- The "heckler" interrupts with short, quick heckles at random intervals.
- The performer must respond with equally quick comebacks, aiming to keep the exchange to 10 seconds or less each time.
- Switch roles after 10 minutes.
- Repeat for 3-4 rounds each.

This exercise hones your ability to think quickly and deliver sharp, concise responses to hecklers.

Escalation Ladder

Setup: Two comedians, one performer and one heckler, plus a moderator (can be one of the participants).

Exercise:

- The performer begins their set.
- The heckler starts with mild interruptions and gradually escalates to more aggressive heckling over time.
- The performer practices appropriate responses, adjusting their approach as the heckling intensifies.
- The moderator calls out different levels of escalation (e.g., "Level 1," "Level 3," "Level 5") to guide the heckler's intensity.
- Switch roles after 15 minutes.

Benefits: This exercise helps comedians practice adapting their responses to different levels of heckling intensity and recognizing when to change tactics.

Audience Ally Simulation

Three or more participants - one performer, one primary heckler, and one or more audience members.

Exercise:

- The performer starts their routine.
- The primary heckler interrupts periodically.
- The performer practices responses that engage the rest of the "audience," seeking their support in handling the heckler.
- The audience members react naturally, sometimes supporting the comedian and sometimes the heckler.
- Rotate roles every 10-15 minutes.

This exercise helps comedians practice crowd control techniques and learn how to enlist audience support when dealing with hecklers.

Improv Integration Challenge

Setup: Two comedians, one performer and one heckler.

Exercise:

- The performer begins their set.
- The heckler interrupts with random, unrelated comments or questions.
- The performer must incorporate the heckler's comments into their routine, creating impromptu jokes or segues.
- Continue for 10 minutes, then switch roles.
- Repeat for 3-4 rounds each.

This exercise develops comedians' improvisational skills and ability to turn unexpected interruptions into comedic opportunities.

Multi-Heckler Mayhem

Setup: One performer and 3-4 other participants acting as hecklers.

Exercise:

- The performer starts their routine.
- Multiple hecklers interrupt at various times, creating a challenging environment.
- The performer practices managing multiple disruptive elements simultaneously, using various techniques to maintain control.
- Rotate the performer role every 10-15 minutes.

Benefits: This exercise prepares comedians for more complex heckling situations and improves their ability to manage a difficult room.

PART 3
FINE-TUNING YOUR ACT

CHAPTER 5

FINE-TUNING YOUR ACT

In the early stages, comedians focus on creating raw material, but experienced ones understand that refinement is a continuous process. This chapter emphasizes the ongoing enhancement of acts to maintain freshness and relevance. Regardless of how long a routine has been performed, subtle adjustments are crucial for establishing meaningful connections with diverse audiences over time.

Effective fine-tuning involves balancing creative risks with respecting foundational elements that build audience comfort and loyalty. Experimentation introduces surprises that keep even long-time fans engaged, while reliability preserves the core essence that retains their loyalty. Thoughtful evaluation guides modifications, whether in wording, structure, or delivery, to adapt to evolving audience expectations.

By meticulously refining punchlines and refining stage presence, comedians sustain their momentum and keep their performances stimulating, preventing routines from becoming repetitive and dull. Regular revision not only reignites performers' passion but also energizes audiences. This chapter offers strategies to elevate material and performances using proven techniques that ensure growth outpaces stagnation, providing ongoing satisfaction to both performers and audiences. Embracing continual learning reinforces comedy as a timeless art form.

Rehearsal Techniques and Tips

While comedy thrives on natural instincts, meticulous routine preparation yields substantial rewards. This section outlines effective methods that amplify the outcomes of rehearsals, from refining words to perfecting personas. Consistent practice consolidates insights, transforming raw ideas into polished, audience-pleasing moments. It emphasizes crucial elements such as setting clear intentions, repetitive practice, video analysis, note-taking, experimental performances, and collaborative feedback.

Dedicated rehearsal turns rough drafts into dynamic, confidence-boosting performances, fostering a deep connection with one's material. Lessons learned during practice sessions create muscle memory, enabling comedians to navigate live performances with ease. Committing to continuous improvement ensures that each performance reaches its full potential, unleashing the strengths of the act consistently.

This approach not only enhances comedic delivery but also cultivates intimacy with the material, allowing comedians to confidently adapt to the unpredictable nature of live shows. It underscores the importance of ongoing mastery in refining performances and delivering memorable experiences for audiences time and again.

Intent-Setting

Setting clear intentions in comedy rehearsal can significantly enhance performance and skill development:

- **Intent-Setting:** Specify goals such as improving set flow or tightening pacing to focus practice efforts effectively.
- **Presence and Poise Under Pressure:** Set intentions to enhance composure during interruptions or increase stage command to refine presence during rehearsals.
- **Memorization and Retention:** Establish goals like memorizing new material without notes by a set date to motivate effective retention strategies.
- **Redirection Technique Mastery:** Intend to sharpen disruption-handling skills through paired exercises to purposefully improve in targeted areas.
- **Rhetorical Experimentation:** Make intentions to try new rebuttal styles for disruptions in journaling to expand techniques and comfort levels beyond the usual norms.
- **Performance Feedback Focus:** Clarify intentions to gather specific feedback on aspects of performances from videotaped sets to benefit set goals and growth.
- **Community Building:** Set goals to foster bonding with diverse comedians through rehearsals to advance the art and enhance versatility in managing disruptions effectively.

Repetition

Repeating material consistently helps engrain it in memory, reducing the need for notes or prompts. This enables performers to focus their full mental energy on engaging the audience without distraction. With practiced recall, spontaneous improvisations and reactions flow more freely, enhancing ease of execution. Through consistent rehearsal, mastery becomes second nature.

Regular repetition reinforces skills, ingraining techniques deeply rather than superficially. This ensures that alternative methods can be effortlessly accessed under pressure, maintaining control in any situation. Over time, consistent practice allows performers to move beyond memorized fallbacks and explore new creative avenues confidently. Habitual practice strengthens the ability to remain lively and adaptable, even in challenging moments, enhancing every performance. Mastery deepens through dedicated and consistent effort, making performances effortlessly enjoyable for all involved.

Video Recording

Recording sessions on video exposes nuances that may go unnoticed during live performances, such as repetitive phrases, pauses, or missed punchlines. Reviewing these recordings with objectivity helps highlight habitual patterns that can be consciously adjusted and improved. Rather than seeking praise, professionals often focus on identifying and refining minor imperfections to optimize their progress continuously.

An observer's perspective through recordings allows performers to see beyond their own experience filters, revealing blind spots that may otherwise be invisible. This insight propels growth by enabling targeted adjustments and enhancements.

Furthermore, reviewing recordings reinforces the effectiveness of techniques and builds confidence in their execution. By observing successful adaptations under pressure, performers gain faith in their crisis management skills and learn to make nuanced adjustments where intuition alone might have sufficed before.

Repeated viewings of recordings inspire and motivate by showcasing the ability to gracefully handle difficulties, encouraging perseverance until mastery feels as natural as breathing. Each review strengthens confidence by focusing on refining techniques and perfecting precision, transforming fleeting moments of success into consistent and deliberate performance excellence.

Notetaking

Journaling about transitions, tags, or sections that need tightening ensures revisions are portable, ready to be refined wherever creativity strikes. This practice prevents ideas from evaporating after leaving the stage. Notes crystallize insights, making it easier to streamline awkward sections upon review and spark improvements whenever inspiration strikes. Documenting both successes and areas for improvement allows acts to evolve continuously, rather than relying on sporadic moments of serendipity.

Handling Disruptions

Recording jottings proves invaluable when facing new disruptions, capturing successful redirection techniques that can be applied to future challenges. Notes preserve effective tactics for managing unique interruptions or sensitive topics, providing a strategic advantage in unpredictable situations. Documenting realizations applies strategy progressively, enhancing resilience before unexpected events. Over time, these annotations cultivate mastery by distilling lessons learned anywhere, facilitating steady progress toward mastering redirection techniques as second nature. Insights gained from deliberate note-taking enrich techniques endlessly through systematic review and application.

Performance Experimentation

Exploring performances in low-pressure environments allows for safe refinement. Making small adjustments in phrasing or stage presence and then gauging audience reactions helps comedians understand nuances that may not be apparent during solitary preparation. Iterative trials in live settings provide valuable insights with minimal risk, allowing acts to strengthen before high-stakes shows. Each adjustment contributes to steady growth and offers lessons that are difficult to learn within the confines of rehearsal alone.

Collaborative Feedback

Engaging in collaborative feedback accelerates improvement exponentially. Sharing ideas and receiving diverse viewpoints helps identify flaws that solo work may overlook. External perspectives often reveal strengths that insiders might miss. By exchanging critiques and suggestions with trusted peers, comedians can develop well-rounded acts that benefit from collective wisdom. This process moves beyond a narrow focus on perceived faults, fostering holistic analyses that elevate performances. Multifaceted consultations strengthen the community, guiding acts through outside guidance and broadening initial perspectives.

Vocal and Movement Analysis

- **Vocal Analysis:** Recording vocal delivery from various perspectives reveals habitual speech patterns, inconsistencies in volume, or tones that need refinement. Reviewing playback helps pinpoint specific vocal traits that influence how the performer is perceived and remembered, facilitating adjustments that enhance engagement and retention.
- **Movement and Posture Review:** Capturing movement and stance from different angles exposes subconscious gestures or positions that may distract viewers. Replaying these recordings ensures that performers maintain poise and use gestures effectively to keep the audience engaged. Micro-adjustments identified through review elevate overall performance quality.
- **Filler Word Identification:** By specifically identifying frequent verbal tics or filler words, performers can focus on tightening their speech for smoother delivery. Scrutinizing these aspects helps eliminate pauses and strengthens the connection with the audience, enhancing fluency and impact.
- **Delivery Mannerisms:** Analyzing smaller details such as tempo, enunciation, or energy expenditure throughout a performance helps identify areas that may detract from effectiveness. Making precise adjustments enhances stage presence and conserves energy, optimizing overall delivery.
- **Feedback Appointments:** Sharing recordings for outside feedback provides valuable perspectives on areas for improvement that may be overlooked when practicing alone. Gathering multidimensional feedback strengthens performances by addressing nuanced aspects that contribute to captivating presentations.

Cold Reading to New Listeners

- **Untrained Perspectives:** Testing routines on newcomers provides valuable insights from outside the industry. Their fresh perspective helps identify sections that may be unclear or unengaging to non-aficionados, guiding adjustments for universal comprehension.

- **Cultural Sensitivity Review:** Seeking feedback from individuals of diverse backgrounds helps identify potential cultural sensitivities that may have been overlooked. Incorporating diverse perspectives enhances the act's ability to resonate across multicultural audiences, ensuring inclusivity and respect.
- **Developmental Editing:** Newcomers often notice pacing issues such as uneven flows or abrupt topic shifts that may disrupt understanding. Addressing these insights through edits improves the act's developmental structure, making it more comprehensible and engaging for all listeners.
- **Language Clarity:** Fresh perspectives clarify ambiguous phrasing, niche terminology, or insider jokes that could alienate outsiders. Adjustments in language simplify communication, broadening the act's appeal to a wider audience.
- **Concept Accessibility:** Validating routines with outsiders ensures that concepts remain interesting and relatable to both non-specialists and aficionados alike. Cold readings optimize engagement universally by ensuring concepts are accessible and compelling across different audience backgrounds and interests.

Character Development

Adding imaginary details to characters anchors abstract concepts, making personalities vivid and relatable. Envisioning their lives beyond the stage adds depth, blending personal and professional backstories to give characters nuanced humanity. These details naturally inspire humorous observations and quirks that keep acts fresh and audiences engaged throughout extended sets.

Developing distinctive catchphrases or repeated mannerisms strengthens characters, embedding them in the public consciousness. These elements can become memes that resonate within the community, ensuring characters are recognized beyond individual performances. Establishing repeatable traits fosters enduring recognition, allowing characters to live on in quotes and allusions across different works.

Creating sturdy frameworks for characters supports their expansion over time, preserving initial creative investments. This approach nurtures concepts with longevity, evolving characters beyond singular performances. Dimensionality in characters fosters deeper audience engagement, as fans proudly support their favorites over the long term.

Environmental Rehearsal

Practicing in future performance venues—whether halls, clubs, or event spaces—involves considering the unique acoustics of each location. These acoustics can alter or dampen vocal tones, the flow of phrases, or the effectiveness of gestures that were refined in more controlled practice environments. Assessing venues ahead of time helps avoid disruptions to tempo or jokes falling flat, allowing performers to adjust techniques to complement each space's specific resonant qualities or limitations.

Factors such as microphone suitability for feedback, audience visibility from the back rows, or surface reflections influence necessary adjustments like volume projection, clear enunciation, or exaggerated facial expressions to ensure engagement regardless of the venue. Rehearsing in various environmental conditions anticipates challenges in maintaining energetic performances and ensuring audience comprehension wherever the act is presented.

Collaborative Run-Throughs

Inviting fellow performers to developmental run-throughs of acts brings objective outside perspectives into play. Their diverse specialties often catch nuances that might be overlooked by someone solely focused on the act. Sharing routines among creatives facilitates an exchange of fresh viewpoints, shedding light on strengths and weaknesses with newfound clarity. This collaborative interplay frequently sparks innovative ideas—such as unexpected callbacks, insightful deconstructions, or enlightening reframings—that might not emerge in solitary practice.

Discussing acts within the community exposes ingrained habits to observant peers who bring different disciplines and angles of critique beyond self-assessment or program analysis alone. Together, these varied critiques pinpoint habitual gestures, cues, or reliance on crutches that may go unnoticed from within. Surrounding oneself with external support prevents stagnation in isolated echo chambers, encouraging transformative growth and stimulating new creative avenues together. Synergy among peers enriches everyone by expanding individual perspectives and fostering collective advancement.

Recording Consistency

Consistently recording performances allows for a longitudinal self-assessment that would otherwise be difficult to achieve. Comparing early versions with current ones highlights the transformational journey with clarity. Progress becomes visible as initial stumbling gives way to effortless mastery over time. Revisiting past recordings also serves as a reminder of where one started, tempering overconfidence with the perspective of how much further there is to go. Importantly, looking back validates efforts, revealing growth that may have felt unseen during the process. Recognizing progress can inspire perseverance and deserves periodic celebration.

Documentation also preserves fleeting successes that might otherwise fade from memory. Reviewing past triumphs reinforces the belief that similar victories are possible in future challenges. Keeping records helps maintain composure during new crises, knowing that difficulties are temporary. Additionally, recordings serve as proof of abilities to oneself and the community, attracting opportunities based on demonstrated past performance.

Seeking and Incorporating Feedback

While comedy's essence springs from natural instincts, refining acts with outside perspectives sharpens them further. This section details productive methods for seeking and integrating reviews that strengthen material. It emphasizes cultivating a variety of advisors, adopting active listening techniques, and prioritizing constructive criticism. By learning to discern valuable insights from less relevant feedback, performers gain the tools to incorporate advice judiciously. Regularly updating perspectives prevents stagnation and fosters evolutionary growth driven by collaborative exchange.

By graciously soliciting feedback and applying insights thoughtfully, comedians build careers fortified by community support. Committing to collaborative growth nurtures longevity by enriching expertise, ensuring that passion and purpose remain vibrant and aligned.

Advisor Diversity

Seeking critiques from advisors representing diverse genders, cultures, ages, and experiences helps identify implicit or systemic biases that might be overlooked within homogeneous circles. Engaging with individuals from different intersections exposes limitations that can result from relying solely on a single perspective. Diverse advisors offer insights that may reveal perspectives overlooked or underrepresented in isolated networks, preventing assumptions that could alienate parts of the intended audience.

Collaborating with advisors from various backgrounds ensures that intersectional perspectives are considered, enhancing the resonance and ethical considerations of creative works through inclusive cross-pollination. Representation fosters further representation, as varied advisors contribute to a deeper understanding and appreciation of diversity.

Together, multidimensional consultations enrich the understanding of diverse perspectives, promoting inclusivity and broadening the reach of creative endeavors.

Active Listening

Nonverbal signals are just as important as what you say. When you make eye contact, nod occasionally, and use phrases like "uh-huh" or "I see," it shows you are paying attention to feedback. These gestures let advisors know you're listening without interrupting them.

Having an open and curious expression, and keeping your arms uncrossed, makes you seem approachable and willing to consider different viewpoints. It's important not to defend or argue until advisors have finished sharing their thoughts. This encourages honest discussions instead of quick explanations.

Asking relevant questions shows you're trying to understand beyond your initial assumptions, which can lead to new insights. Whether you take notes in your head or on paper, it shows you value their feedback beyond just being polite.

At the end of the conversation, thanking them for their time and feedback reinforces openness to honesty and can lead to better collaboration. Active listening isn't just about hearing words – it's about engaging with your eyes, body language, questions, and most importantly, having an open mind without being defensive. This kind of receptiveness helps everyone involved grow and improve.

Prioritizing Constructive Criticism

It's important to distinguish between feedback that promotes growth and criticism that doesn't help. Productive advice provides lessons that can be applied to improve one's work, while mean-spirited or vague comments are not useful. Feedback that comes from empathy and understanding, aimed at helping someone get better, is the most valuable. Superficial or unhelpful remarks don't lead to meaningful progress.

Giving priority to feedback that treats artists and their work with kindness and respect ensures that the criticism itself supports positive development. Similarly, staying polite and open-minded even when faced with unhelpful criticism sets an example of constructive behavior. This encourages potential advisors to offer their best feedback in return. Avoiding defensiveness fosters thoughtful discussions, as reacting harshly can discourage future honest feedback.

By focusing on advice that provides lessons rather than protecting one's ego, and by maintaining empathy throughout, criticism becomes actionable rather than adversarial. This approach establishes conversations that lead to the strongest work through empathetic guidance from all perspectives.

Requesting Specifics Politely

When receiving feedback that suggests areas for improvement, it's helpful to politely ask for specifics to better understand how to proceed. Asking, "Could you give me a specific example of what you mean?" shows that you're actively listening and directs the conversation towards actionable insights.

Requesting examples focuses the feedback on clear weaknesses that can be addressed, rather than vague criticisms that aren't helpful. It encourages advisors to clarify their points in a way that supports improvement.

Maintaining a polite tone fosters thoughtful responses and keeps the interaction positive. Asking for substantiation ensures that critiques are useful and provide a clear direction for improvement, rather than leaving you with unclear feedback that doesn't lead to progress.

Acknowledging Appreciatively

Showing appreciation for an advisor's insights is crucial for maintaining a positive relationship. Thanking them sincerely for their time, perspective, and thoughtful input reinforces that their contributions are valued beyond just providing critique. This approach encourages open and honest feedback, knowing that such honesty supports growth rather than creating resentment.

It's important to express thanks without being defensive, even when receiving criticisms. This prevents unintentionally dismissing their feedback. Acknowledging feedback broadens your perspective, even if you don't adopt all of their suggestions.

Concluding discussions by appreciating both the points that resonated and the discussion process itself helps avoid overlooking any viewpoints. Recognizing what was meaningful and showing respect for the exchange prevents reacting defensively.

Thanking advisors for fostering new conversations encourages openness for future dialogues, benefiting everyone through open-minded and sometimes challenging interactions. Gratitude helps ease tensions, reinforces the core goals of improvement, and motivates ongoing commitment from all involved, ensuring that critiques lead to positive outcomes and strengthened relationships.

Implementation Deliberation

While the desire to improve quickly can lead to immediate adjustments, thoughtful consideration ensures constructive evolution without disrupting the work. Taking time to evaluate each suggestion's merits and how they can practically be integrated helps avoid hasty overcompensation.

Considering critiques within the broader context of previous efforts helps maintain a consistent flow that has been refined through experience. Careful reflection on how modifications can enhance existing strengths ensures continuity that appeals to invested audiences.

Avoiding notes that lead to repetitive changes or inconsistent shifts in persona helps maintain a focused trajectory. It's important to prune suggestions that might distract from solid foundations, retaining core elements while making deliberate enhancements. This approach allows for steady progress rather than erratic changes.

Self-Evaluation Consistency

Regularly asking for feedback from others keeps your work from getting stale. Careers are ongoing journeys that need constant improvement to stay fresh and relevant. When artists ask for feedback at different times, they can find problems before they become habits. Change takes time and persistence, not just one review. Checking yourself often helps you adapt to changing tastes and stay creative. It's also a way to celebrate your successes and stay motivated. By checking in regularly, creators can see where they're doing well and where they can try new things.

Getting feedback regularly keeps you open to growth. It's easier to fix problems early than to find big issues later. Checking periodically helps avoid big surprises when problems have built up over time. Consistent check-ins keep progress steady and inspiration flowing. Reflecting regularly helps you keep improving instead of just relying on past successes. Change is ongoing, so it's important to keep improving consistently.

Reiteration and Openness

Welcoming balanced and constructive feedback regularly is key to celebrating achievements and avoiding complacency. Artists who consistently seek critiques hold themselves accountable to high standards and remain open to improvement. By embracing both positive praise and constructive criticism, they prevent stagnation and continuously grow. Being open to feedback requires humility, which is essential for personal and professional development. Embracing advice with gratitude ensures that progress remains ongoing.

Using Multimedia for Feedback

Engaging with a variety of sources such as in-person advisors, online surveys, social media followers, and test audiences provides a well-rounded perspective. Each source offers unique value: technologists bring digital expertise, while trusted advisors reveal blind spots. Diverse viewpoints enrich understanding and expand creative possibilities. Interacting across different platforms and mediums exposes artists to new ideas and stimulates innovative thinking. Incorporating wide-ranging feedback strengthens the impact and relevance of their work.

Consistency Across Feedback Sources

Analyzing recurring feedback themes across evaluations highlights the most critical areas for improvement. Addressing core issues promptly removes barriers to success and fosters meaningful changes. While feedback providers may differ, consistent themes often indicate where focused efforts are needed for significant improvements. Recognizing these patterns streamlines decision-making and guides strategic reforms, promoting coherence and progress.

Enhancing Creative Growth through Accountability and Collaboration

1. **Resolution Accountability**: Acknowledge and thank reviewers for their insights, communicating how feedback has been incorporated to show tangible improvements. Transparency builds confidence and maintains rapport with advisors, demonstrating their crucial role in fostering ongoing growth.

2. **Iteration Documentation**: Document changes over time through updates and transitions, engaging communities in the developmental journey. Sharing evolutions showcases progress, inspires others, and fosters long-term followership and guidance within creative networks.
3. **Comedian Peer-Groups**: Foster competitive yet supportive peer groups committed to improvement through honest feedback. Diverse perspectives prevent tunnel vision, encouraging collaboration and multiple income streams. Peer partnerships evolve into lifelong learning-focused alliances, navigating professional challenges collectively.
4. **Outside-Field Consultants**: Collaborate with consultants from different fields to bring fresh insights and bridge understanding across mediums. Their diverse perspectives challenge assumptions, fuel innovation, and open doors to new professional opportunities, enhancing career scopes.
5. **Establishing Office Hours**: Dedicate regular time slots for feedback, ensuring accessibility and preventing advisor overwhelm. Even brief check-ins contribute valuable insights, demonstrating a commitment to inclusivity and diverse viewpoints. Prioritizing accessibility fosters compassion and understanding through shared experiences.
6. **Celebrating Feedback Incorporation**: Publicly recognize advisors for their contributions and highlight integrated suggestions to energize communities and inspire ongoing collaboration. Personal acknowledgments of impact establish genuine connections and goodwill, nurturing future partnerships.
7. **Advisory Transparency**: Share works-in-progress openly and seek unfiltered feedback to foster trust and transparency. Authentic dialogue transforms critics into allies, guiding continued improvement and risk-taking. Transparency builds mutual ownership of successes and strengthens relationships through shared challenges.

Refining Your Material for Success

Embracing the Iterative Process

Refining comedy material is an ongoing, iterative process that requires patience, persistence, and a willingness to experiment. Successful comedians understand that even their best jokes can be improved with time and practice. Take, for example, Dave Chappelle's evolution of his "Racial Draft" sketch. Initially performed on Chappelle's Show in 2004, Chappelle continued to refine and expand on this concept in his stand-up specials over the years, most recently in his 2019 Netflix special "Sticks & Stones."

To embrace this iterative process, start by recording all your performances, no matter how small the venue. In 2023, rising comedian Sarah Chen made waves with her "100 Sets Challenge," where she performed and recorded 100 sets in 100 days, meticulously analyzing each performance to refine her material. This intense focus on iteration allowed her to rapidly improve her timing, delivery, and content.

Remember, refinement isn't just about changing words or punchlines. It's about understanding the rhythm of your jokes, the pacing of your set, and the overall flow of your performance. As comedy legend Jerry Seinfeld once said, "It's not the joke, it's the joker." Your unique voice and perspective are what truly make your material stand out.

Leveraging Technology for Feedback

In the digital age, comedians have access to unprecedented tools for gathering feedback and refining their material. Social media platforms like TikTok and Instagram have become testing grounds for new material. In 2024, comedian Hasan Minhaj gained attention for his "Joke Lab" series on TikTok, where he would post different versions of the same joke and use audience engagement metrics to refine his material.

Audio analysis tools have also become invaluable for comedians looking to perfect their timing and delivery. The AI-powered app "LaughTrack," launched in 2023, uses machine learning algorithms to analyze the volume and frequency of audience laughter during a performance. This data can help comedians identify which parts of their set are working well and which need improvement.

However, it's important to remember that technology should complement, not replace, live performance experience. As veteran comic Maria Bamford notes, "There's no substitute for the energy of a live audience. But these tools can help us understand that energy better."

Tailoring Material to Your Audience

Successful comedians understand that different audiences respond to different types of material. Refining your act isn't just about improving individual jokes, but about crafting sets that resonate with specific audiences.

One effective technique for tailoring material is the "City Specific" joke. This involves crafting jokes or references that are unique to the city or region where you're performing. For example, when performing in Seattle, you might reference the city's famous rain or coffee culture. This shows the audience that you've put effort into understanding their local context.

Another approach is to use "Flexible Framing." This involves having multiple setups or contexts for the same punchline, allowing you to adjust your joke to fit different audiences. Comedian John Mulaney is known for this technique, often reframing his jokes to appeal to different age groups or cultural backgrounds.

Embracing Failure as a Learning Opportunity

Perhaps the most crucial aspect of refining your material is learning to embrace failure. Every comedian, no matter how successful, has bombed on stage. The key is to view these moments not as defeats, but as valuable learning experiences. In his 2024 masterclass on comedy, Chris Rock revealed that he still regularly performs at small clubs to test new material, knowing that some of it will inevitably fail.

One technique for turning failure into success is the "Post-Mortem Analysis." After a set that didn't go well, take time to break down what happened. Was it the content of the jokes? The delivery? The audience's mood? By systematically analyzing your failures, you can identify patterns and areas for improvement.

Another approach is the "Fail Fast" method. This involves intentionally trying out new, risky material early in your set. If it fails, you can quickly move on to more proven material. If it succeeds, you've discovered a new gem to refine further. As comedy legend Joan Rivers once said, "I succeeded by saying what everyone else is thinking."

Push Procrastination and Get Booked

Procrastination is a common hurdle for comedians, often rooted in fear of failure or perfectionism. In the comedy world, where rejection and criticism are part of the journey, it's easy to fall into the trap of endless preparation without taking action.

Creating a Strategic Action Plan

To push past procrastination and get booked, it's crucial to have a clear, actionable plan. In 2024, rising comedian Jake Chen made waves with his "Comedy Career Blueprint" approach, which he credits for his rapid success in the industry.

Chen's method involves breaking down the goal of "getting booked" into smaller, manageable tasks. For example:

1. Write 5 new minutes of material each week
2. Perform at 3 open mics per week
3. Reach out to 2 new venues or bookers each month
4. Update social media content 3 times per week
5. Attend 1 networking event per month

By setting specific, measurable goals, you create a roadmap for success and make the process less overwhelming.

Another effective strategy is the "Time-Blocking Technique," used by comedians like John Mulaney. This involves dedicating specific blocks of time to different aspects of your comedy career. For instance, 9-11 AM for writing, 2-4 PM for outreach and networking, and evenings for performances.

Remember to make your plan flexible and adaptable. As veteran comic Maria Bamford advises, "The comedy landscape is always changing. Your plan should be a living document that evolves with your career."

Leveraging Technology to Streamline Booking Processes

In the digital age, technology can be a powerful ally in pushing past procrastination and getting booked. Many comedians are now using specialized apps and platforms to streamline their booking processes.

For example, the app "GigFinder," launched in 2023, uses AI algorithms to match comedians with suitable venues based on their style, experience level, and location. Comedian Sarah Silverman, an early adopter of the app, credits it with helping her book 30% more shows in 2023 compared to the previous year.

Social media platforms are also evolving to better serve performers. In 2024, Instagram introduced its "Performer Showcase" feature, allowing comedians to highlight their best clips and easily connect with potential bookers. Within six months of its launch, over 10,000 comedians reported booking gigs through this feature.

Another useful tool is "BookedIn," a calendar and contract management app designed specifically for performers. It simplifies the often tedious process of managing multiple bookings, sending invoices, and tracking payments.

While these tools can be incredibly helpful, it's important not to let them become another form of procrastination. As comedian Patton Oswalt warns, "Don't spend so much time optimizing your systems that you forget to actually write jokes and get on stage."

Building a Supportive Network

Pushing past procrastination and getting booked often requires a strong support system. Surrounding yourself with motivated peers can provide accountability, encouragement, and valuable connections.

In 2023, a group of Los Angeles-based comedians formed the "Hustle & Joke Collective," a supportive community dedicated to helping each other achieve their comedy goals. Members set weekly targets, share resources, and even attend each other's shows to provide feedback and moral support.

Another effective networking strategy is the "Coffee Challenge," popularized by comedian and podcaster Joe Rogan. The challenge involves reaching out to one industry contact each week and inviting them for coffee. This low-pressure approach to networking has helped many comedians build valuable relationships with bookers, club owners, and fellow performers.

Online communities can also be powerful networking tools. The Facebook group "Comics Helping Comics," with over 50,000 members as of 2024, has become a go-to resource for comedians looking for gig opportunities, advice, and moral support.

Remember, networking isn't just about what others can do for you. As comedy legend Steve Martin advises, "Be so good they can't ignore you." Focus on honing your craft and being a supportive member of the comedy community, and opportunities will often follow.

Overcoming Rejection and Maintaining Momentum

In the pursuit of getting booked, rejection is inevitable. The key is to not let it derail your progress. Successful comedians view rejection as a natural part of the process, not a reflection of their worth or potential.

Comedian Amy Schumer, in her 2024 masterclass on comedy, shared her "Rejection Reframe" technique. After each rejection, she asks herself, "What can I learn from this?" and "How can I improve for next time?" This approach turns rejections into opportunities for growth rather than reasons to procrastinate.

Another powerful tool is the "100 No's Challenge," popularized by comedian and motivational speaker Jia Jiang. The idea is to actively seek out rejection 100 times, desensitizing yourself to the fear of "no" in the process. Many comedians have adapted this technique, setting goals to reach out to 100 bookers or apply to 100 festivals, regardless of the outcome.

Maintaining momentum is crucial in pushing past procrastination. The "Don't Break the Chain" method, famously used by Jerry Seinfeld, involves marking a calendar for each day you work towards your comedy goals. The growing chain of marked days becomes a powerful motivator to keep going.

Remember, every "no" brings you closer to a "yes." As Joan Rivers once said, "In comedy, you persevere or you die." Keep pushing forward, learning from each experience, and success will come.

Exercises: Solo Rehearsal Exercises for Perfecting Delivery; Pair Exercises for Giving and Receiving Feedback on Material

Solo Rehearsal Exercises for Perfecting Delivery

The Mirror Technique

Duration: 30-45 minutes

Setup: Stand in front of a full-length mirror with a microphone or mic-like object.

Exercise:

- Perform your entire set as if you're on stage.
- Pay close attention to your facial expressions, body language, and gestures.
- Focus on maintaining eye contact with yourself throughout the performance.
- After each joke, pause to assess your delivery and make mental notes for improvement.
- Repeat the process, consciously adjusting your delivery based on your observations.

This exercise helps you become more aware of your physical presence on stage and allows you to fine-tune your non-verbal communication.

The Recording Critique

Duration: 1 hour (including performance and review)

Setup: Use a camera or smartphone to record yourself performing your set.

Exercise:

- Set up the camera and perform your entire set as if you're in front of a live audience.
- Watch the recording, taking notes on your timing, pacing, and delivery.
- Pay special attention to filler words, unnecessary pauses, or distracting mannerisms.
- Repeat the process, focusing on improving the areas you identified.
- Compare recordings over time to track your progress.

This exercise provides an objective view of your performance and helps you identify areas for improvement that you might miss in the moment.

The Pacing Drill

Duration: 20-30 minutes

Setup: Choose a short segment of your set (2-3 minutes) and a timer.

Exercise:

- Perform the segment at your normal pace, timing yourself.
- Now, perform the same segment 25% faster than your normal pace.
- Next, perform it 25% slower than your normal pace.
- Finally, perform it at what you feel is the optimal pace based on your experiments.
- Repeat this process with different segments of your set.

This exercise helps you find the optimal pacing for your jokes and trains you to adjust your timing on the fly.

The Accent Challenge

Duration: 15-20 minutes

Setup: Choose a short bit from your set (1-2 minutes).

Exercise:

- Perform the bit in your normal voice.
- Now, perform the same bit in various accents or character voices (e.g., British, Southern, robot, etc.).
- Pay attention to how the changes in voice affect your timing and emphasis.
- Incorporate any insights gained back into your normal delivery.

This exercise helps you explore different aspects of vocal delivery and can lead to new insights about emphasis and timing.

The Distraction Resistance Drill

Duration: 15-20 minutes

Setup: Choose a 5-minute segment of your set and some form of background distraction (TV, radio, or a playlist of random sounds).

Exercise:

- Start your background distraction at a low volume.
- Begin performing your set, focusing on maintaining your concentration and timing.
- Gradually increase the volume of the distraction.
- Continue your performance, adjusting as necessary to maintain your focus and delivery.

This exercise helps you develop the ability to stay focused and maintain your performance quality even in distracting environments.

Pair Exercises for Giving and Receiving Feedback on Material

The Laugh-O-Meter

Duration: 30 minutes per person (including performance and feedback)

Setup: Two comedians, one performer and one audience member/critic.

Exercise:

- The performer delivers their set.
- The audience member reacts naturally but also keeps a "laugh log," noting:
  - Which jokes got the biggest laughs
  - Which jokes fell flat
  - Where the energy dipped or peaked
- After the set, the audience member provides detailed feedback based on their laugh log.
- Switch roles and repeat.

This exercise provides specific, quantifiable feedback on joke effectiveness and overall set structure.

The Punch-Up Workshop

Duration: 30-40 minutes

Setup: Two comedians with prepared material.

Exercise:

- Comedian A performs a joke or short bit.
- Comedian B listens, then offers 2-3 alternative punchlines or tags for the joke.
- Comedian A tries out these suggestions.
- Discuss which versions work best and why.
- Switch roles and repeat with Comedian B's material.

This exercise helps comedians explore different angles for their jokes and learn to collaborate on punch-ups.

The Premise Expansion Challenge

Duration: 20-25 minutes per premise

Setup: Two comedians with a list of premises or topic ideas.

Exercise:

- Comedian A presents a premise.
- Both comedians take 5 minutes to independently write as many jokes or angles on that premise as possible.
- Share and compare the results, discussing which approaches seem most promising.
- Collaborate to combine and refine the best ideas.
- Switch to Comedian B's premise and repeat.

This exercise stimulates creativity, helps generate new material, and provides insight into different comedic approaches.

The Constructive Critique Swap

Duration: 45 minutes per person (including performance and feedback)

Setup: Two comedians with 10-minute sets prepared.

Exercise:

- Comedian A performs their set.
- Comedian B takes notes, focusing on three categories:
  - Strengths (what worked well)
  - Opportunities (areas for improvement)
  - Suggestions (specific ideas for enhancing the material)
- Comedian B provides feedback using the "feedback sandwich" method (strength, opportunity, strength).
- Discuss the feedback, with Comedian A asking clarifying questions.
- Switch roles and repeat with Comedian B's set.

This exercise provides structured, balanced feedback and practices both giving and receiving constructive criticism.

The Character Perspective Shift

Duration: 30 minutes

Setup: Two comedians with prepared material.

Exercise:

- Comedian A performs a joke or short bit.
- Comedian B suggests a specific character or perspective to retell the joke from (e.g., a child, an alien, a historical figure).
- Comedian A attempts to rework and perform the joke from this new perspective.
- Discuss how the perspective shift affects the joke and if it reveals any new angles.
- Switch roles and repeat with Comedian B's material.

This exercise encourages flexible thinking and can help comedians discover new dimensions to their material.

PART 4
MARKETING YOURSELF AS A STAND-UP COMIC

CHAPTER 6

MARKETING YOURSELF AS A STAND-UP COMIC

Starting out as a stand-up comedian is thrilling but can also be overwhelming. Besides writing and perfecting your jokes, you'll need to focus on promoting yourself effectively. It's important to get your name out there so you can build an audience and find opportunities to perform. This chapter will give you strategies and tips to promote your comedy career.

We'll cover using social media wisely, connecting with other comedians in your area, creating good promotional materials like photos and business cards, and actively booking shows whenever you can. Whether you're new to open mic nights or aiming to advance in your career, the advice here can help more people discover your comedy. With a good plan, you can spend less time on promotion and more on crafting jokes that will make audiences laugh.

Building Your Brand as A Comedian

Building a strong brand is crucially important for any aspiring comedian hoping to establish a successful career in comedy. In an industry where attracting audiences and standing out from the competition is key, having a clear brand identity provides focus to one's promotional efforts and gives fans an idea of what to expect from a comedian's act. This section will explore the various elements that go into branding oneself as a comedian. It will discuss topics such as defining one's comedic style and persona, using social media effectively, developing quality promotional materials, networking within the industry, and strategizing show bookings. With purposeful effort given to cultivating a memorable brand, up-and-coming comedians can connect with more fans and progress to bigger career opportunities.

Defining Your Comedic Style and Persona

Deciding on a Comedic Style

Before seriously working on branding themselves, comedians first need to gain clarity on the specific style or type of comedy they want to pursue. The most common styles include observational humor, character-based comedy, political/current events humor, relatable everyday jokes, or offensive/boundary-pushing material. Determining a focus helps shape the tone of one's act and branding. Having an authentic comedic voice is more important than trying to be all things to all people.

Your Onstage Personality

Along with style, defining one's onstage persona is equally crucial for branding purposes. Effective comedians cultivate stage characters through exaggerated traits of their real-life personalities. Fans respond well to comedians with distinctive onstage energies like high-energy and hyper or deadpan and dry. Comedians can also brand themselves through lifestyle associations like being intellectual or crude. Developing a distinct character translates to the branding feeling consistent from live shows to promotional materials.

Refining Through Practice and Feedback

Of course, a comedian's style takes shape gradually over time through experimenting with different material at open mic nights and honing act through the feedback of club owners and other comedians. Smart comedians record their earliest shows to critically self-assess their pacing, energy levels, and persona consistency. They also actively seek critique to pinpoint strengths and refocus areas needing polish before branding around a definable comedic identity. Even famous comedians continued tweaking their style behind the scenes for years as their careers progressed.

Using Social Media Effectively

Establishing an Online Presence

In today's digital world, having a strong social media presence is crucial for any young comedian hoping to self-promote and build an audience. The first step is setting up professional profiles on major platforms like Facebook, Twitter, Instagram and YouTube or LinkedIn. Consistency is key, so comedians should devote regular time each week toward social media engagement. It's important for profiles to match the comedian's brand through customized designs, bios highlighting their style and background, and posting schedules that suit each platform.

Creating Shareable Content

To establish an engaged online following, comedians need to provide high-quality, shareable original content on a consistent basis. This includes posting clips of stand-up sets, behind-the-scenes photos and videos, comedy articles they write, and lifestyle updates giving fans insight into their personalities. Since visual content like photos and videos tend to perform best across social platforms, comedians benefit from learning basic video editing and photography skills. Finding a balance of promotional and casual, personality-driven content keeps profiles feeling lively and followers interested.

Building an Email List

While active on major social networks, comedians should also prioritize growing an opt-in email list on their website. Capturing email addresses at live shows, through social media sign-up forms or a lead magnet ebook gives direct contact with fans. Regular email newsletters allow comedians to share longer-form updates and exclusive content while directly promoting upcoming shows. A strong email list proves invaluable for driving ticket sales and spreading upcoming opportunities to a dedicated following.

Taking Advantage of Social Advertising

Once comedians build engaged profiles and a following, doubling down through paid social media marketing can significantly boost their brands. Platforms like Facebook and Instagram offer advertising options to promote specific shows or podcast/YouTube channel appearances. With tested targeting skills, comedians can reach larger audiences and attract new fans beyond their current circles. Viewing social media as an investment in the business of comedy allows ambitious performers to take their brands national and even global.

Producing Quality Promotional Materials

Developing Headshots and Bios

Traditional promotional materials still hold merit even in the digital age. Comedians need high-quality professional headshots showcasing their brand image through wardrobe, hair/makeup choices and backgrounds matching their comedic personalities. They also require concise yet compelling bios highlighting their style, influences, past shows and accolades. When done well, headshots and bios leave positive first impressions at agent/talent buyer showcases and boost Google search authority.

Designing Business Cards and Posters

Simple yet attention-grabbing printed collateral enhances brand awareness. Nice business cards with headshot, website and social media links get distributed to other comedians, club owners and potential fans. Teasers/posters promote specific shows, while branded postcards provide a unique giveaway. For variety, some comedians print stickers or temporary tattoos as promotional items. Developing stationery templates proves cost-effective and produces consistent branding for all physical materials.

Creating Branded Swag

Highly popular comedians sustain engagement through branded merch. While overdone swag risks appearing inauthentic or desperate for income, certain items compliment artists' brands such affordable shirts, hats, buttons, pins and drink koozies. Up-and-comers can also consider branded stickers, temporary tattoos and even specialty items like drink coasters. Quality, affordability and relevance to the comedic identity keep swag feeling like value-added perks, not cheesy come-ons.

Launching Websites and Email Signups

Comedians require carefully developed websites as online headquarters for their brands. Beyond quality headshots, bios and video clips, sites feature merchandise sales, email signup forms, show calendars and comic's latest articles/blogs. Search engine optimization boosts traffic, and ease of navigation with mobile responsiveness builds usability. sites convert casual viewers into dedicated new email subscribers and social followers, further extending an comic's brand reach.

Networking Within the Industry

Developing Local Industry Relationships

For comedians starting out, building relationships within their local comedy scenes proves extremely valuable. Actively attending open mic nights introduces them to other up-and-comers as well as seasoned club owners and talent bookers. Coming across polite, hardworking and willing to assist with shows earns respect. Volunteering to emcee also brings experience dealing with live audiences. Gradually, a reputation develops of being dedicated to both stand-up improvement and scene involvement.

Joining a Talent Agency

As skills, experience and fanbases grow, representation by reputable agencies allows access to larger shows. While some book directly, agencies take percentages in exchange for pitching clients to clubs, colleges and corporate events. Comedians ready to work full circuits seek agencies matched to their brands and experience levels for optimal exposure. Positive client reviews through agency association further raises comedians' profiles.

Attending Industry Conferences and Open Calls

Select national comedy festivals accept applications by comics serious about career advancement. Panels teach marketing while showcase competitions get live feedback from industry judges. Invitations open doors at top clubs and networks looking to discover talent. Comedians maximize exposure through charismatic elevator pitches at festivals alongside flawless showcase sets elevating their brands.

Appearing on Podcasts and as Radio Guests

Guesting on established comedian-hosted podcasts expands recognition among hardcore fans nationwide. It also grants opportunities discussing career journeys, creative processes and industry insights. Getting booked requires coming across down-to-earth through digital outreach in addition to crafted comedic personas. Satellite radio channels, morning shows and podcasts also uplift careers through interviews tapping comedians as entertainment commentators.

Strategizing Show Bookings

Performing Locally on Weeklies and Pop Ups

Success starts at home through consistent weekly booked spots in addition to locally arranged specialty shows. Well-booked comedians balance veteran headliners with growing undercards through fair compensation. These low-pressure weekly slots build local following before expanding to out-of-towners. Comedians coordinate occasional pop-up room takeovers, variety and fundraising shows, hosting duties developing all-around entertainment values.

Securing Spots at Out-of-Town Festivals and Clubs

Booking travel commitments sees comedians growing regionally through college gigs as well as spots at allied regional comedy clubs and festivals. Research ensures multi-slot bookings across several close states making trips worth costs and time away. Comedians use warm host venues re-bookings, gaining loyalty and buzz carrying brands further afield. Strategic social media promotion ties faraway shows to ever-growing home followings.

Applying for TV Writing Jobs, Specials and Videos

Comedians secure representation assisting larger acts in addition to pitching personal projects to top comedy outlets. Applying for sitcom and late-night writing staffs gives invaluable experience collaborating with professionals.

Utilizing Social Media and Online Platforms

In the digital age, social media and online platforms have become indispensable tools for stand-up comedians looking to build their brand, connect with audiences, and advance their careers. The landscape is constantly evolving, with new platforms and features emerging regularly, offering fresh opportunities for comedians to showcase their talent and engage with fans.

Crafting a Cohesive Online Persona

Your online presence should be an extension of your on-stage persona. Consistency across platforms helps build a strong, recognizable brand. Take Ali Wong, for example. Her Instagram feed seamlessly blends her bold, unapologetic comedy style with glimpses of her personal life as a mother and wife. This cohesive online persona has helped her cultivate a loyal following that extends beyond her stand-up performances.

To create your own cohesive online persona:

- Identify 3-5 key aspects of your comedic style or personality

- Ensure these elements are reflected in your content across all platforms

- Use consistent profile pictures, bios, and handles across platforms

Remember, authenticity is key. As comedian Patton Oswalt advises, "Don't try to be someone else online. Your unique voice is your biggest asset."

Leveraging Platform-Specific Features

Each social media platform offers unique features that can be leveraged for comedy content. Understanding and utilizing these features can significantly boost your online presence.

TikTok, for instance, has become a powerhouse for comedic content. The platform's short-form video format and robust editing tools are perfect for quick jokes and sketches. Comedian Kris Siddiqi gained over 500,000 followers in 2023 with his "Everyday Afterlife" series, which uses TikTok's green screen effect to humorously depict mundane activities in the afterlife.

On Instagram, the Stories feature allows for more casual, behind-the-scenes content. Comedian Celeste Barber has mastered this, often using Stories to share funny commentary on her daily life, which complements her popular celebrity parody posts.

Twitter remains a valuable platform for sharing quick jokes and engaging with fans. In 2024, Hannah Gadsby's witty, often political tweets have become as much a part of her brand as her stand-up specials.

Creating Shareable Content

In the world of social media, shareable content is king. The more your content is shared, the wider your reach becomes. But what makes content shareable?

Relatability is a key factor. Comedian Taylor Tomlinson's Instagram reels about dating and mental health in your 20s regularly go viral because they tap into common experiences of her millennial and Gen Z audience.

Another strategy is to create content that encourages interaction. In 2023, John Mulaney launched a successful "Finish the Joke" series on Twitter, where he would post the setup to a joke and invite followers to provide punchlines. This not only increased engagement but also provided him with a wealth of material to potentially incorporate into his act.

Remember, not every post needs to be a fully formed joke. Behind-the-scenes content, relatable observations, or even posts about your comedy process can all be highly shareable if they resonate with your audience.

Utilizing Video Platforms

While traditional social media platforms are valuable, dedicated video platforms offer unique opportunities for comedians to showcase longer-form content.

YouTube remains a powerhouse for comedy content. Many comedians use it to post clips from their specials, behind-the-scenes content, or even full-length shows. In 2024, Ronny Chieng launched a successful YouTube series called "Cooking with Comedians," where he interviews fellow comics while attempting to cook dishes from their cultural backgrounds. This not only showcases his comedy but also helps him connect with a wider audience.

Twitch, traditionally associated with gaming, has seen an influx of comedians in recent years. Steve Hofstetter, for example, regularly streams on Twitch, performing stand-up and interacting directly with his audience. This real-time interaction offers a unique way to test new material and build a dedicated fan base.

Engaging with Your Audience

Social media isn't just about broadcasting your content; it's about building a community. Engaging with your audience can turn casual viewers into dedicated fans.

Respond to comments, participate in discussions, and show appreciation for your followers. Comedian Aparna Nancherla is known for her witty responses to fan comments on Twitter, which often become content in themselves.

Consider hosting Q&A sessions or live streams to interact directly with your audience. In 2023, Bo Burnham hosted a series of Instagram Live sessions where he answered fan questions and even workshopped new material, creating a sense of exclusivity and connection for his followers.

Measuring and Adapting

The beauty of digital platforms is the wealth of data they provide. Use analytics tools to understand what content resonates with your audience and when they're most active online.

Comedian Iliza Shlesinger credits her rapid rise in popularity partly to her meticulous analysis of social media metrics. She uses this data to inform not just her online content, but also her stand-up material, ensuring she's always in tune with her audience's interests.

Remember, the digital landscape is always changing. Stay informed about new platforms and features, and be willing to experiment. As Chris Rock once said, "In comedy, you have to keep changing up. The moment you're comfortable, you're not funny anymore."

By effectively utilizing social media and online platforms, stand-up comedians can significantly expand their reach, build a loyal fan base, and create new opportunities for their career. The key is to approach these platforms strategically, always keeping your unique comedic voice at the forefront.

Booking Gigs and Networking in The Comedy Industry

In the competitive world of stand-up comedy, booking gigs and networking are essential skills that can make or break a comedian's career. The landscape of the comedy industry is constantly evolving, with new venues, formats, and opportunities emerging regularly. Successful comedians understand that their job extends far beyond writing and performing jokes – it's about building relationships, creating opportunities, and navigating the business side of comedy.

The first step in successfully booking gigs and networking is understanding the various players in the comedy ecosystem. This includes club owners, bookers, promoters, agents, managers, and fellow comedians. Each of these roles plays a crucial part in a comedian's career trajectory.

Mastering the Art of the Follow-Up

One of the most crucial skills in booking gigs and networking is the art of the follow-up. Many opportunities are lost simply because comedians fail to maintain contact after initial meetings.

In 2024, comedian John Mulaney shared his early career strategy: "After every show, I'd email the booker thanking them for the opportunity and expressing interest in future spots. I kept a spreadsheet of all my contacts and made sure to touch base every few months, even if just to share a recent achievement."

Effective follow-up strategies include:

- Sending a thank-you note or email after each gig
- Sharing updates about your career milestones
- Offering to help with future shows or events

However, it's important to strike a balance. As booker Lisa Wong cautions, "There's a fine line between persistent and annoying. Make your follow-ups meaningful and respectful of the recipient's time."

Leveraging Technology for Booking and Networking

The digital age has transformed how comedians book gigs and network. Numerous apps and platforms have emerged to streamline these processes.

For example, the app "GigFindr," launched in 2023, uses AI algorithms to match comedians with suitable venues based on their style and experience level. Comedian Aparna Nancherla reported booking 40% more shows in her first six months of using the app.

Social media platforms also play a crucial role. LinkedIn, often overlooked by comedians, has become a valuable tool for connecting with industry professionals. In 2024, comedian Hasan Minhaj revealed that he landed his first major TV writing gig through a LinkedIn connection.

Other useful tech tools include:

- Calendly for easy scheduling of meetings and gigs
- Hootsuite for managing social media presence across platforms
- Zoom for virtual networking events and online shows

Creating Your Own Opportunities

In today's comedy landscape, waiting to be discovered is no longer a viable strategy. Successful comedians are increasingly creating their own opportunities.

Take the case of Ali Wong, who in 2023 launched her own comedy festival, "Wong's Way," featuring up-and-coming Asian American comedians. This not only provided a platform for emerging talent but also solidified Wong's position as a tastemaker in the industry.

Other ways to create opportunities include:

- Starting a comedy podcast to showcase your humor and network with guests
- Organizing local comedy shows or open mics
- Creating and promoting virtual comedy events

As comedian Tig Notaro once said, "Don't wait for permission to be funny. Create the spaces where you can shine."

Building a Strong Personal Brand

In the crowded comedy market, a strong personal brand can set you apart and make you more bookable. Your brand should encompass your unique comedic voice, your online presence, and your professional reputation.

Comedian Taylor Tomlinson's meteoric rise is a testament to the power of branding. Her relatable content about life in your 20s, consistently delivered across stand-up, social media, and her podcast, has made her instantly recognizable and highly sought after for gigs.

To build your personal brand:

- Identify your unique comedic perspective
- Ensure consistency across all platforms and performances
- Develop a professional press kit including a compelling bio, high-quality photos, and performance clips

Remember, as Chris Rock advises, "Your job is to be so good, so unique, that they can't ignore you."

Networking Beyond the Comedy Club

While comedy clubs remain important, successful comedians know the value of networking beyond traditional comedy spaces.

In 2024, Dave Chappelle made headlines by performing at tech industry conferences, opening up a whole new market for high-paying corporate gigs. Similarly, Ali Wong's collaboration with fashion brands has expanded her reach and booking opportunities beyond the comedy world.

Other networking opportunities to consider:

- Attending film and TV festivals
- Participating in charity events
- Engaging with local businesses for potential sponsorships or unique venue opportunities

As Jimmy Carr once quipped, "Comedy is everywhere. Your job is to find the stages that others overlook."

Exercises: Solo Brainstorming Sessions for Personal Branding; Pair Exercises for Networking Practice

Solo Brainstorming Sessions for Personal Branding

The Core Values Exploration

Duration: 30-45 minutes

Exercise:

- Start by listing 20-30 words that you feel describe you or your comedy.
- Narrow this list down to the 10 most resonant words.
- From these 10, choose the top 5 that you believe best represent your core values as a comedian.
- For each of these 5 words, write a short paragraph explaining how it relates to your comedy and personal brand.
- Finally, try to distill your brand into a single sentence using these core values.

Sarah Chen, a rising comedian known for her observational humor about millennial life, distilled her brand to: "Hilariously honest storytelling that turns everyday anxieties into shared laughter."

This exercise helps you identify and articulate the fundamental aspects of your comedic persona and brand.

The Audience Avatar Creation

Duration: 30 minutes

Exercise:

- Imagine your ideal audience member. Give them a name and age.
- Describe their background, interests, and sense of humor.
- What are their pain points or frustrations that your comedy addresses?
- What kind of entertainment do they typically enjoy?

- Where do they hang out online and offline?
- Write a short paragraph from their perspective explaining why they love your comedy.

Dave Chappelle once described his ideal audience member as "someone who's not easily offended, loves social commentary, and isn't afraid to laugh at uncomfortable truths."

This exercise helps you tailor your brand and marketing efforts to reach and resonate with your target audience.

The Brand Mood Board

Duration: 45 minutes

Materials: Large paper or digital canvas, images (from magazines or online), markers

Exercise:

- Collect images, colors, fonts, and words that represent the feel of your comedy brand.
- Arrange these elements on your paper or digital canvas to create a visual representation of your brand.
- Include elements that represent your comedy style, target audience, and career aspirations.
- Write a short description of what each element represents and why you included it.

Ali Wong created a mood board featuring bold colors, images of working mothers, and Asian American cultural references, which helped shape her stage presence and marketing materials.

This visual exercise helps you crystallize the look and feel of your brand, which can inform your promotional materials, social media presence, and even stage attire.

The Unique Selling Proposition (USP) Generator

Duration: 30 minutes

Exercise:

- List 5-10 comedians who inspire you or whom you're often compared to.

- For each, write down what makes them unique or successful.
- Now, list what makes you different from each of these comedians.
- Based on these differences, craft 3-5 potential USPs for yourself.
- Refine these into a single, powerful USP that encapsulates your unique comedic offering.

Hannah Gadsby's USP could be described as "Challenging the conventions of stand-up comedy through deeply personal, thought-provoking storytelling."

This exercise helps you identify and articulate what makes you stand out in the crowded comedy landscape.

The Future Bio Visualization

Duration: 30 minutes

Exercise:

- Imagine it's five years in the future and you've achieved significant success in comedy.
- Write a detailed bio for this future version of yourself.
- Include specific accomplishments, your style of comedy, and how you're perceived in the industry.
- Now, work backwards. What steps would you need to take to make this bio a reality?
- Use these steps to create a rough five-year plan for your comedy career and personal brand development.

In 2018, Phoebe Waller-Bridge might have visualized her future bio as including "Emmy-winning creator and star of groundbreaking comedy series," which became reality with Fleabag's success.

This exercise helps you set concrete goals for your personal brand and career, providing direction for your branding efforts.

Pair Exercises for Networking Practice

The Elevator Pitch Exchange

Duration: 20 minutes

Exercise:

- Each comedian prepares a 30-second "elevator pitch" about their comedy and brand.
- Take turns delivering your pitches to each other.
- Provide feedback on clarity, engagement, and memorability.
- Refine your pitches based on the feedback.
- Practice delivering the refined pitches in different tones (enthusiastic, casual, professional) to prepare for various networking scenarios.

This exercise helps you articulate your brand quickly and effectively in networking situations.

The Mock Industry Mixer

Duration: 30 minutes

Exercise:

- Create character cards for industry roles (club owner, talent agent, podcast host, etc.).
- Take turns role-playing these characters and networking with each other.
- Practice introducing yourself, discussing your comedy, and finding common ground.
- After each interaction, provide feedback on what worked well and what could be improved.

Jerry Seinfeld once shared that he practiced his networking skills at actual industry events by challenging himself to make one meaningful connection each time.

This exercise helps you prepare for real networking events and practice adapting your approach to different industry professionals.

The Social Media Strategy Swap

Duration: 30 minutes

Exercise:

- Each comedian shares their current social media strategy and goals.
- Brainstorm 5-10 content ideas for each other that align with your respective brands.
- Discuss potential collaborations or cross-promotion opportunities.
- Provide constructive feedback on each other's online presence and suggest improvements.

Comedians like Jaboukie Young-White have built their brands largely through clever, consistent social media presences.

This exercise helps you refine your social media strategy and explore collaborative opportunities.

The Mutual Connection Web

Duration: 25 minutes

Exercise:

- Each comedian lists 10 key contacts in their network (other comedians, industry professionals, etc.).
- Compare lists and identify any mutual connections or potential introductions you could make for each other.
- Role-play making these introductions, practicing how you'd describe each other to a third party.
- Discuss strategies for maintaining and leveraging these network connections.

This exercise helps you realize the value of your existing network and practice making meaningful introductions.

The Feedback Loop Challenge

Duration: 30 minutes

Exercise:

- Each comedian shares a recent networking success and a networking challenge they're facing.
- Discuss the factors that contributed to the success and brainstorm solutions for the challenge.
- Role-play implementing these solutions in a networking scenario.
- Provide feedback on each other's approach and suggest refinements.
- Create accountability plans to implement these networking strategies in real-life situations.

This exercise helps you learn from each other's experiences and develop strategies to overcome networking challenges.

PART 5
MASTERING THE CRAFT OF COMEDY

CHAPTER 7

THE FUNDAMENTAL ELEMENTS OF EXCELLENT HUMOR

C omedy is a complex artform that relies on careful crafting to resonate with audiences. While humor is highly subjective, there are certain fundamental elements that consistently contribute to jokes, routines, and performances that are widely considered excellent. This chapter will break down these core components of humor writing and delivery that many successful comedians utilize in their work. Exploring techniques like timing, observational humor, exaggeration, understatement, irony, and self-deprecation can offer emerging comics practical tools to incorporate into their own material and improve their skills. Understanding these fundamental elements is an important first step for any comedian seeking to take their humor to the next level through sophisticated joke construction and skilled delivery.

Analyzing What Makes Jokes and Punchlines Work

Creating jokes that consistently make people laugh is a skill that requires a lot of practice and learning. Comedy is different for everyone, but successful joke writers often use specific techniques to make their punchlines work well. This section will explore the usual structural parts and psychological aspects that research shows help humor be effective. By understanding how setups, choosing subjects, timing, and other principles affect how people react to jokes, new comedians can analyze and improve their own material. Breaking down what makes professional comedians' jokes connect with people is a crucial step toward getting better at making people laugh yourself.

Examining Joke Formats

Many famous comedy routines follow specific, well-tested structural patterns. Here are some popular formats:

1. Setup → Punchline:

- This format begins with a brief setup followed by a surprising conclusion.
- The punchline catches the audience off guard, maximizing comedic timing.
- The simplicity of this structure delivers humor efficiently and directly.

2. Question → Answer:

- This format poses a problem that implicitly demands a solution.
- The punchline cleverly subverts expectations, creating humor from the gap between anticipated and actual responses.

- Delaying the "aha!" moment heightens the enjoyment of the punchline.

3. Situation → Complication:

- Starting with a familiar, everyday scenario grounds the audience.
- The twist into absurdity from an initially peaceful situation amplifies laughter through relatability.
- This format plays on the contrast between normalcy and unexpected chaos.

4. Contrast:

- This format exploits the humor in contrasting two vastly different images or ideas.
- Pairing the ordinary with the outrageous tickles both logic and the instinct for rebellious humor.
- It disrupts stable associations in a delightfully surprising manner.

5. Callbacks:

- Repurposing running jokes or references throughout a performance rewards attentive listeners.
- Callbacks enhance audience engagement by evolving jokes and deepening the connection between performer and crowd.
- They demonstrate comedic versatility by revisiting themes and creating a sense of continuity.

Analyzing Subject Selection

Choosing the right comedy subjects involves considering target audiences and current cultural trends. Here are key factors that influence how well topics resonate:

1. Relatability:

- Jokes about common experiences and human quirks resonate universally.
- Laughter often stems from recognizing shared humanity in others, fostering intimacy between performer and audience.

2. Comfort Level:

- It's important to gauge audience comfort and avoid topics that may alienate early on.
- Balancing subject matter and intensity maintains energy without causing offense, ensuring a positive rapport.

3. Accessibility:

- Memorable jokes are easily understood without needing too much explanation.
- Simple concepts facilitate laughter more effectively than complex ideas that distract from the humor.

4. Novelty:

- Fresh perspectives and creative angles keep familiar topics engaging and prevent predictability.
- Innovating within well-trodden themes maintains audience interest and enhances comedic impact.

5. Specificity:

- Detailed storytelling, vivid characters, and sensory descriptions bring jokes to life.
- Creating mental images helps audiences connect more deeply with the humor, turning abstract ideas into relatable and humorous anecdotes.

Tailoring comedy material using these insights helps comedians consistently entertain diverse audiences with humor that resonates deeply. By choosing subjects that are relatable, respectful of comfort levels, accessible, novel, and specific, comedians can enhance their comedic delivery and connect more effectively with their fans.

Mastering Timing Principles

Timing in comedy includes rhythm, pacing, and how jokes are delivered effectively. Here are some concepts to understand:

1. Setup Duration:

- A setup that's too short can confuse the audience or not set up the joke properly.

- If the setup is too long, it can make the audience lose interest before the punchline.
- Finding the right balance engages listeners fully.

2. Pauses:

- Strategic pauses in speech build suspense and anticipation for the punchline.
- Well-timed silences make the punchline more satisfying by creating expectations and then surprising them.
- Pauses make the moment of laughter feel more rewarding.

3. Delivery Speed:

- Changing how fast or slow you speak, the rhythm of your voice, and how you stress words can make punchlines stand out or catch people off guard.
- Adjusting these elements fine-tunes the timing of jokes to make them more satisfying.
- The way jokes are delivered controls how people react and laugh.

4. Layering:

- Building up the setup in stages adds depth and complexity to the joke.
- This technique prepares the audience for a bigger, more surprising punchline that requires them to think a bit more.
- Layering makes jokes more satisfying and complete in people's minds.

5. Reworking:

- Testing jokes in front of live audiences helps figure out which setups and punchlines work best together.
- Trying different ways of delivering jokes helps find the best timing and rhythm for maximum laughs.
- Timing gets better as comedians experiment and see what works best on stage.

Understanding and using these timing techniques can greatly increase the comedic impact of any joke. Timing isn't always visible, but it's crucial for making people laugh and enjoy the show.

Understanding The Role of Exaggeration and Contrast

Exaggeration and contrast are two fundamental tools in a comedian's arsenal, serving as powerful mechanisms to amplify humor and engage audiences. These techniques, when skillfully employed, can transform mundane observations into hilarious narratives and create memorable comedic moments.

The Art of Exaggeration

Exaggeration in comedy involves taking a truth or a relatable situation and pushing it to its logical extreme. This technique works by creating a gap between reality and the exaggerated scenario, with the humor often lying in the absurdity of this gap.

In recent years, comedians have been pushing the boundaries of exaggeration to new heights. Take for example John Mulaney's bit about his childhood fear of quicksand. He exaggerates this common childhood misconception to absurd levels, imagining a world where quicksand is a daily threat:

"I always thought quicksand was going to be a much bigger problem than it turned out to be. Because if you watch cartoons, quicksand is like the third biggest thing you have to worry about in adult life behind real sticks of dynamite and giant anvils falling on you from the sky."

This exaggeration works because it takes a relatable childhood fear and blows it out of proportion, creating a humorous contrast between childhood expectations and adult reality.

Another master of exaggeration is Dave Chappelle. In his recent specials, he often takes societal issues and exaggerates them to highlight their absurdity. For instance, in his bit about the opioid crisis, he exaggerates the contrast between how society treats different drug epidemics:

"If you're white and you're addicted to opioids, it's a 'health crisis'. If you're black and you're addicted to crack, it's a 'crime wave'."

Here, Chappelle uses exaggeration to underscore the racial disparities in how drug addiction is perceived and treated, turning a serious issue into a thought-provoking comedic bit.

The Power of Contrast

Contrast in comedy involves juxtaposing two disparate ideas, situations, or characters to create humor. This technique works by subverting expectations and creating cognitive dissonance that resolves in laughter.

Ali Wong masterfully uses contrast in her comedy, often juxtaposing her Harvard education with crass humor and discussions of bodily functions. This contrast between high and low creates a comedic tension that resonates with audiences.

In her special "Baby Cobra," Wong contrasts the expectations of her Asian heritage with her actual behavior:

"I think it's very rare and unusual to see an Asian-American woman talk about her sexuality in a very open way. And I think that's why a lot of Asian men hate on me... They're like, 'How dare she talk about her sexuality? That's not what we do. We're supposed to be submissive and quiet.'"

Here, the contrast between cultural expectations and Wong's bold, outspoken style creates humor while also making a point about cultural stereotypes.

Another comedian who excels at using contrast is Hannah Gadsby. In her groundbreaking special "Nanette," Gadsby contrasts the expected structure and content of a comedy special with serious, personal revelations. This dramatic contrast not only creates moments of tension and release but also challenges the very nature of stand-up comedy.

Combining Exaggeration and Contrast

When exaggeration and contrast are used together, they can create particularly potent comedy. Bill Burr often combines these techniques in his rants about everyday annoyances. In a bit about people who bring their dogs everywhere, he exaggerates the idea of emotional support animals to absurd levels:

"You know what my emotional support animal is? It's an AR-15. Every time I feel anxious in public, I just fire off a few rounds, and suddenly, I've got all the space I need."

Here, Burr exaggerates the concept of emotional support to an extreme (an assault rifle) and contrasts it with the usual cuddly animals associated with emotional support, creating a darkly humorous take on a current trend.

The Risks and Rewards

While exaggeration and contrast can be powerful tools, they also come with risks. Push too far, and the joke can become unrelatable or offensive. The key is to find the sweet spot where the exaggeration or contrast is surprising and humorous, but still grounded enough in reality for the audience to connect with.

For example, Anthony Jeselnik is known for his extremely dark humor that often pushes the boundaries of taste. His jokes frequently use extreme exaggeration and stark contrasts to shock the audience:

"My girlfriend loves to eat chocolate. She's always eating chocolate, and she likes to joke she's got a chocolate addiction. 'Get me away from those Hersheys bars. I'm addicted to them.' It's not funny. It's not funny at all. I put my hand in her purse to get the car keys, and I pulled out three syringes full of Hershey's syrup."

This joke works for Jeselnik's audience because they expect and appreciate his boundary-pushing style. However, the same joke might fall flat or offend in a different context.

As society becomes more complex and nuanced, comedians are finding new ways to use exaggeration and contrast to comment on current events and social issues. For instance, Hasan Minhaj in his show "Patriot Act" used exaggerated visuals and stark contrasts to make complex topics like the stock market or immigration policy both understandable and funny.

Moving forward, we can expect to see comedians using these techniques in increasingly sophisticated ways, potentially incorporating technology like augmented reality or interactive elements to enhance their exaggerations and contrasts.

The Importance of Word Choice And Delivery

In the world of stand-up comedy, the difference between a laugh and silence often comes down to two critical elements: word choice and delivery. These components are the building blocks of a comedian's craft, transforming raw ideas into polished jokes that resonate with audiences.

The Power of Precise Word Choice

Word choice in comedy is an art form in itself. The right word can elevate a joke from mediocre to memorable, while the wrong one can cause a punchline to fall flat. Comedians often spend hours agonizing over individual words, understanding that each one carries weight and potential for humor.

George Carlin, renowned for his mastery of language, once said, "I love words. I thank you for hearing my words." Carlin's famous "Seven Words You Can Never Say on Television" routine demonstrates the power of word choice. By focusing on specific, taboo words, Carlin created a routine that was both shocking and thought-provoking, challenging societal norms through careful word selection.

In recent years, comedians have continued to push the boundaries of word choice. Hannah Gadsby, in her groundbreaking special "Nanette," uses precise language to deconstruct the very nature of comedy:

"I have built a career out of self-deprecating humor. And I don't want to do that anymore. Because do you understand what self-deprecation means when it comes from somebody who already exists in the margins? It's not humility. It's humiliation."

Here, Gadsby's choice of "humiliation" instead of "humility" transforms the sentence from a simple statement into a powerful commentary on the nature of marginalized voices in comedy.

The Rhythm of Language

Beyond individual word choices, the rhythm and flow of language play a crucial role in comedy. Comedians often craft their jokes with an ear for the musicality of speech, understanding that the right cadence can enhance the impact of a punchline.

John Mulaney, known for his precise and polished delivery, often uses repetition and rhythm to build humor. In his bit about a prostate exam, he repeats the phrase "new in town" with varying emphases:

"I'm new in town, and it gets worse. I'm new in town, and it gets worse. I have AIDS. I'm new in town. I have AIDS. I'm new in town. And I'm gay."

The repetition and gradual reveal create a rhythm that builds tension and releases it in bursts of laughter, demonstrating how word choice and arrangement can amplify humor.

The Role of Delivery

Even the most perfectly crafted joke can fall flat if not delivered correctly. Delivery encompasses a range of factors including timing, tone, facial expressions, and body language.

Timing, often called the backbone of comedy, refers to the precise moment a punchline is delivered. Too early, and the audience might not be ready; too late, and the moment passes. Dave Chappelle, a master of timing, often uses pauses to build tension before a punchline. In his recent specials, he's known to take long pauses, allowing the audience's anticipation to build before delivering the joke.

Tone and inflection can completely change the meaning of words. Consider the difference between saying "Great" sarcastically versus enthusiastically. Comedians like Sarah Silverman often play with tone, delivering dark or controversial material in a cheerful, almost naive tone for comedic effect.

Physical Delivery

Body language and facial expressions are crucial components of delivery that can enhance or even replace verbal punchlines. Sebastian Maniscalco is renowned for his exaggerated facial expressions and physical comedy. His bit about people showing up uninvited to your house relies heavily on his physicality:

"Nobody comes to your house anymore. Remember that? People would just show up. [Makes a shocked face and gestures wildly] 'Hey! What are you doing here?'"

The humor in this bit comes as much from Maniscalco's exaggerated reactions as from his words, demonstrating the power of physical delivery in comedy.

Adapting to the Audience

One of the most challenging aspects of word choice and delivery in stand-up comedy is the need to adapt to different audiences. A joke that kills in New York might bomb in rural Texas, not necessarily because of the content, but because of how it's presented.

Ali Wong, in her specials, often adjusts her delivery when discussing her Asian heritage, exaggerating or downplaying her accent depending on the joke and the presumed audience. This flexibility in delivery allows her to connect with a wide range of viewers while maintaining her unique voice.

The Impact of Technology

In recent years, technology has begun to play a role in both word choice and delivery. With the rise of social media, comedians are learning to craft jokes that work both on stage and in tweet form. This has led to a trend of more concise, punchy jokes that can easily be shared online.

Additionally, streaming specials have changed how some comedians approach delivery. With viewers able to pause, rewind, and rewatch at will, some comedians are crafting more densely packed jokes, rewarding attentive viewers with layers of humor that might not be caught in a single viewing.

The Intersection of Word Choice and Delivery

While word choice and delivery are often discussed separately, the reality is that they're deeply interconnected. The words a comedian chooses inform their delivery, and their delivery style influences their word choice.

Take Bo Burnham's special "Inside," created during the COVID-19 pandemic. Burnham's word choice is precise and often ironic, but it's his delivery - isolated in a room, often breaking the fourth wall - that gives the words their full impact. In his song "White Woman's Instagram," the lyrics alone are funny, but it's Burnham's deadpan delivery and the visual representations that elevate the piece to a brilliant commentary on social media culture.

As society evolves, so too does the language of comedy. Comedians today are finding new ways to play with words and delivery to address complex topics like gender, race, and political polarization.

Exercises: Solo Analysis of Comedic Techniques in Famous Jokes; Pair Exercises for Practicing Delivery and Timing with Emphasis on Key Comedic Elements

Solo Analysis of Comedic Techniques in Famous Jokes

Exercise 1: Deconstructing the Punchline

Duration: 30 minutes

Materials: Selection of 5-10 famous jokes from various comedians

Steps:

1. Choose a famous joke and write it down.
2. Identify the setup and punchline.
3. Analyze why the punchline works:
   - What expectation does the setup create?
   - How does the punchline subvert this expectation?
   - What specific words make the punchline effective?
4. Try rewriting the punchline using different words. How does this change the joke's impact?
5. Repeat with other jokes, comparing techniques used.

Example: Let's take Mitch Hedberg's famous joke: "I used to do drugs. I still do, but I used to, too."

- Setup: "I used to do drugs."
- Punchline: "I still do, but I used to, too."
- Analysis: The setup creates an expectation that the speaker has quit drugs. The punchline subverts this by revealing he still does drugs. The effectiveness lies in the unexpected addition "but I used to, too," which plays with the concept of time and the phrase "used to."

Exercise 2: Identifying Comedic Devices

Duration: 45 minutes

Materials: Video clips of stand-up performances

Steps:

1. Watch a 5-minute clip of a stand-up performance.
2. Pause after each joke and identify the main comedic device used (e.g., exaggeration, contrast, misdirection, callback).
3. Note how the comedian's delivery enhances the chosen device.
4. Analyze how the comedian transitions between jokes and maintains a cohesive set.
5. Repeat with clips from different comedians, comparing styles.

Example: In a clip from Ali Wong's "Baby Cobra," you might identify:

- Exaggeration in her description of pregnancy symptoms
- Contrast between her Harvard education and crass humor
- Callbacks to earlier jokes about her husband

Exercise 3: Rhythm and Timing Analysis

Duration: 30 minutes

Materials: Audio recordings of stand-up performances

Steps:

1. Listen to a 3-minute segment of a stand-up routine.
2. Mark the pauses and emphasize stressed words.
3. Analyze the rhythm:
   o How does the comedian use pauses for effect?
   o Where do they speed up or slow down their delivery?
4. Try reading the joke aloud, mimicking the comedian's rhythm.
5. Experiment with changing the rhythm. How does this affect the joke's impact?

Example: Analyzing Dave Chappelle's delivery, you might notice:

- Long pauses before punchlines to build tension
- Quicker delivery during setup to maintain engagement
- Emphasis on specific words to guide the audience's attention

Pair Exercises for Practicing Delivery and Timing

Exercise 1: The Emphasis Shift

Duration: 20 minutes

Steps:

1. Choose a short, simple joke.
2. Take turns delivering the joke, each time emphasizing a different word.
3. Discuss how changing the emphasis alters the joke's meaning or impact.
4. Try delivering the joke with exaggerated pauses in different places.
5. Reflect on which delivery felt most effective and why.

Example Joke: "I'm not saying I'm Wonder Woman, I'm just saying no one has ever seen me and Wonder Woman in the same room together."

Exercise 2: The Tone Transformation

Duration: 30 minutes

Steps:

1. Select a news article or formal text.
2. Take turns reading it aloud in different comedic tones (e.g., sarcastic, overenthusiastic, deadpan).
3. Observe how tone changes the perception of the content.
4. Challenge each other to find humor in the text through delivery alone.
5. Discuss which tones worked best for different types of content.

Exercise 3: The Tag Team

Duration: 25 minutes

Steps:

1. Comedian A starts telling a story or joke.
2. At any point, Comedian B can tag in and continue the story.
3. Focus on maintaining flow and adding humorous elements.
4. After the exercise, discuss:

- o How did you build on each other's ideas?
- o Where did you find opportunities for humor?
- o How did you maintain consistent characters or themes?

Exercise 4: The Callback Challenge

Duration: 40 minutes

Steps:

1. Each comedian performs a 2-minute set.
2. Together, identify potential callbacks in each set.
3. Perform the sets again, this time incorporating callbacks to each other's material.
4. Discuss how the callbacks affected the flow and cohesion of the combined set.

Exercise 5: The Contrast Conundrum

Duration: 30 minutes

Steps:

1. Choose a mundane topic (e.g., making toast, tying shoelaces).
2. Comedian A describes the topic in an overly dramatic, intense manner.
3. Comedian B interjects with extremely underwhelmed, deadpan responses.
4. Switch roles and repeat with a new topic.
5. Reflect on how the contrast in delivery styles created humor.

Exercise 6: The Exaggeration Escalation

Duration: 25 minutes

Steps:

1. Start with a simple statement about an everyday annoyance.
2. Take turns exaggerating the statement, each time making it more extreme.
3. Focus on using specific, vivid language and varied delivery techniques.
4. Continue until you can't escalate further.
5. Discuss at what point the exaggeration was most effective and why.

Example Start: "I hate it when people chew loudly."

These exercises will help comedians develop a deeper understanding of comedic techniques and improve their delivery and timing. By analyzing famous jokes and practicing with a partner, comedians can refine their skills and discover new ways to enhance their material. Remember, the key to improvement is consistent practice and a willingness to experiment with different techniques.

CHAPTER 8

STEPS AND PROCEDURES FOR CREATING MATERIAL

Creating original comedy material is essential for any aspiring comedian. While learning techniques from humor icons and using established structures is valuable, every comedian needs to develop their own unique voice and collection of jokes. This chapter will outline a structured process for new comedians to systematically generate fresh jokes and routines. By following clear steps and engaging in exercises to refine their material, beginners can start creating sets ready for stage performances.

A thoughtful and iterative creative approach helps comedians authentically express their unique perspectives and comedic talents. Regular writing sessions, using proven formulas, help streamline the materialization of ideas. With dedication and persistence, aspiring comedians can build a repertoire of funny bits that truly reflect their authentic selves.

Step-By-Step Guide to Generating Comedy Ideas

Creating new comedy material consistently is essential for professional comedians, but it can be a daunting task. This section offers aspiring comedians a structured process to systematically brainstorm and refine new joke ideas. Following clear steps helps streamline creativity and uncover each comedian's unique comedic style. Regular sessions using proven techniques build a growing collection of jokes that resonate with shared human experiences. With guidance and a commitment to routine ideation, any dedicated performer can maximize their natural wit for audience enjoyment.

Establish a Regular Writing Routine

Creating dedicated time for creativity enhances productivity:

1. Scheduled Brainstorming Sessions:

- Allocate distraction-free periods weekly for generating ideas.
- Blocking focused creative time on your calendar ensures consistent output rather than relying on sporadic inspiration.

2. Setting Achievable Goals:

- Aim for small, manageable goals, like crafting 3-5 potential jokes per hour.
- Attainable targets maintain momentum and make the writing process enjoyable, avoiding burnout from excessive quotas.

3. Varying Routines:

- Keep brainstorming sessions fresh by alternating between free-flowing idea generation and structured exercises.
- Switching up approaches stimulates creativity and prevents monotony over time.

4. Conditioning Observance:

- Regular writing habits train your mind to notice everyday humor.
- Cultivate an ever-expanding collection of comedic material by journaling humorous observations and absurdities in daily life.

Prompt the imagination with random inspiration

Being creative means letting go of strict mental rules. Here are some ways to get creative:

- Start by writing jokes about everyday objects or things around you. Don't worry about making sense at first.
- Make short jokes about what's happening in the news or popular topics. Find funny observations or jokes.
- Think about emotions, hobbies, or made-up situations that could be funny. Be curious and explore different ideas, even if they seem strange.

By being open to unexpected ideas and following your curiosity, you can find new and funny ways to look at things.

Experiment with Common Joke Formats

Try experimenting with different types of jokes. For example, you can use simple setups followed by punchlines for quick, observational humor. One-liners are another classic format to try. Callback jokes are great for surprising twists or clever comments that catch people off guard. Sharing personal stories can also be funny, letting you turn everyday experiences into laughs. You can even use props or games to involve your audience more. By starting with these well-known joke styles, you can build your comedic skills step by step. As you get more comfortable, you can add your own style and expand your material. Experimenting with different formats is a fun way to get better at making people laugh.

Revisit and Refine Ideas Repeatedly

In creating comedy, it's crucial to keep refining your ideas to make them as good as they can be. Here are some techniques:

1. **Take breaks:** Put aside your joke drafts and come back to them later with a fresh perspective.
2. **Try different punchlines:** Experiment with alternate punchlines for the same setup to find the funniest match.
3. **Adjust details:** Tweak the wording, emphasize different parts, or change the context to see what gets the best laughs.
4. **Test out loud:** Read your drafts aloud multiple times to perfect the timing and flow.
5. **Combine ideas:** Merge separate jokes that explore similar themes to strengthen your overall message.

By continuously refining your jokes through these methods, you'll sharpen your setups and punchlines, improve the structure, and keep your humor engaging and fresh. Dedication to this process allows jokes to evolve into their most effective and memorable forms.

Categorize and Organize Material

Efficiently organizing your comedic ideas helps you access a wealth of creativity accumulated over time. Here's how:

1. **Transcribe and categorize:** Write down each idea, whether on paper or digitally, and categorize it with metadata like type (observational, anecdotal, parody), source, length, and keywords. This makes it easier to find later.
2. **Partition by type:** Organize ideas by their typical forms (like observational humor, personal anecdotes, or parodies) to match them with different performance opportunities.
3. **Use a digital repository:** Store all your ideas in a central cloud-based digital repository. This allows you to edit and access notes from any device, anytime, and encourages building on older ideas that might have been overlooked.
4. **Organize by runtime:** Group drafts according to their potential length, which helps when preparing for performances of varying durations.
5. **Review periodically:** Regularly revisit your stored ideas to rediscover gems that might have been forgotten. This fresh perspective can breathe new life into older concepts.

By maintaining disciplined filing and cataloging habits, you can quickly unearth a treasure trove of comedy ideas to fuel creativity during brainstorming sessions.

Extract Feedback and Expand Horizons

Outside input enhances growth:

- Swap jokes with comedian peers for objective analysis fresh takes.
- Incorporate direction from mentors critiquing areas needing polish.
- Study comedy across cultures appreciating universals translating specifics.
- Remain teachable through failures by gleaning what did and didn't land why.
- Stay vigilant noticing what humor evolves into as cultural tides ebb and flow.

The iterative active practicing of these techniques efficiently generates aptitude for spurring new concepts to explore comedy's endless possibilities. Regular routines make implicit skills to steadily develop stronger individualized comedic voices. Commitment reaps myriad returns via an evergreen well of intriguing material nourishing to share.

Structuring Jokes and Punchlines

The Anatomy of a Joke: Setup and Punchline

At its core, every joke consists of two main components: the setup and the punchline. The setup creates an expectation or tension, while the punchline subverts that expectation in a surprising, humorous way. Understanding this basic structure is crucial for crafting effective jokes.

The setup should provide just enough information to lead the audience in a particular direction, without giving away the joke. It's about creating a scenario or premise that the audience can easily grasp. The key is to be concise and clear, avoiding unnecessary details that might distract from the punchline.

The punchline, on the other hand, is where the magic happens. It should be unexpected, yet somehow logical within the context of the setup. The best punchlines often rely on a twist or reinterpretation of the setup that catches the audience off guard.

For example, consider this classic joke by Mitch Hedberg:

- Setup: "I used to do drugs."
- Punchline: "I still do, but I used to, too."

Here, the setup leads us to believe Hedberg is about to share a story about his past drug use. The punchline subverts this expectation by revealing he still uses drugs, with the added twist of the redundant "used to" creating an amusing logical loop.

Structuring for Maximum Impact: The Rule of Three and Tags

Two additional techniques that can enhance your joke structures are the Rule of Three and the use of tags.

The Rule of Three is a classic comedy writing technique that involves listing three items, with the third being the comedic payoff. The first two items establish a pattern, and the third breaks it unexpectedly. This structure is effective because it creates a rhythm that the audience subconsciously recognizes, making the punchline even more impactful when it breaks that rhythm.

Consider this example from Tina Fey:

- "I have a new philosophy. I'm only going to dread one day at a time."

Here, we expect three positive items after "philosophy," but the third item ("dread") subverts this expectation, creating the punchline.

Tags are additional punchlines that follow the main punchline of a joke. They can extend the laugh and squeeze more humor out of a single premise. John Mulaney often uses tags effectively in his comedy.

For example:

Main joke: "I was once on the phone with Blockbuster Video, which is a very old-fashioned sentence."

- Tag 1: "That's like when your Grandma dies and you're like, 'She died in a Blockbuster.'"

- Tag 2: "That's like if I said, 'I got into a fight with a hoop and a stick.'"

Each tag builds on the concept of outdated references, extending the humor of the original joke.

Crafting Long-Form Comedy: Storytelling and Escalation

While short, punchy jokes have their place, many modern comedians are embracing long-form comedy, particularly through storytelling and escalation techniques.

Storytelling in comedy involves weaving jokes and humorous observations into a larger narrative. This approach can keep an audience engaged for extended periods and allows for more complex setups and payoffs. Comedians like Mike Birbiglia and Hannah Gadsby have gained recognition for their ability to blend humor with poignant storytelling.

To craft effective comedy stories:

1. Start with a compelling premise or personal experience.
2. Pepper your story with jokes and humorous observations.
3. Build towards a significant payoff or revelation.
4. Use callbacks within the story for added cohesion.

Escalation involves starting with a relatively normal premise and gradually taking it to absurd levels. This technique can turn a simple observation into an extended bit. Comedian Tig Notaro is known for her ability to take a simple premise and explore it to increasingly absurd depths, finding new layers of humor as she goes.

For example, a bit might start with a simple observation about disliking small talk, then escalate to imagining increasingly bizarre ways to avoid it, culminating in an absurd scenario like faking your own death every time someone asks "How are you?"

By mastering these various structures and techniques, comedians can craft jokes and routines that are not only funny but also engaging and memorable. The key is to experiment with different approaches, find what works best for your comedic voice, and continually refine your material based on audience reactions.

Expressing Material with The Right Technique

Mastering Timing and Delivery

Timing is often referred to as the heartbeat of comedy. It's not just about what you say, but how and when you say it. Mastering timing involves understanding the rhythm of your jokes, knowing when to pause for effect, and recognizing the perfect moment to deliver your punchline.

One key aspect of timing is the use of pauses. A well-timed pause can build anticipation, allowing the audience's imagination to work and making the punchline even more impactful when it lands. Dave Chappelle is a master of the pregnant pause, often taking long breaks before delivering a punchline to build tension and make the release (laughter) even more powerful.

For example, in one of his routines about encountering a baby on a street corner at 3 AM, Chappelle sets up the joke, then pauses, allowing the audience to imagine the absurdity of the situation before he delivers the punchline:

- "Hey, baby! Baby, what are you doing out here at 3 AM? Go home!"

Delivery, on the other hand, involves the way you express your material vocally. This includes your tone, pitch, volume, and speed. Varying these elements can add depth to your performance and highlight key aspects of your jokes. For instance, a whisper can draw the audience in, while a sudden shout can punctuate a punchline for maximum effect.

Consider how Bo Burnham uses vocal variety in his musical comedy. He often switches between a soft, conversational tone and loud, energetic singing to create contrast and emphasize his punchlines.

Body Language and Stage Presence

Your physical presence on stage is a crucial part of your comedic expression. Body language, facial expressions, and how you use the stage space can significantly enhance your material and even become a source of humor in itself.

Facial expressions are particularly powerful in comedy. A raised eyebrow, a deadpan stare, or an exaggerated look of shock can sometimes be funnier than words. Sebastian Maniscalco is known for his expressive face and often uses exaggerated expressions to punctuate his observational humor about social situations.

For example, in his bit about people showing up uninvited to your house, Maniscalco doesn't just describe the awkwardness verbally. He physically acts out the stiff, uncomfortable body language and facial expressions of someone trying to hide their annoyance, adding an extra layer of humor to the joke.

How you use the stage is also important. Moving with purpose can help emphasize points or act out scenarios. Some comedians, like Robin Williams, were known for their energetic stage presence, using the entire space to bring their rapid-fire comedy to life. Others, like Steven Wright, create humor through contrast by remaining almost stationary while delivering absurd observations.

Developing Your Comedic Voice and Persona

Your comedic voice is your unique perspective and style of humor. It's what sets you apart from other comedians and makes your material distinctively yours. Developing a strong, authentic comedic voice is crucial for connecting with audiences and standing out in the competitive world of stand-up.

Your comedic voice is influenced by your personal experiences, worldview, and what you find funny. It's not something you can force or fake – it needs to be a genuine expression of who you are. Hannah Gadsby's groundbreaking special "Nanette" was powerful largely due to its raw authenticity and willingness to be vulnerable on stage. Gadsby's comedic voice, which blends humor with social commentary and personal revelation, has reshaped perceptions of what stand-up comedy can be.

To develop your comedic voice:

1. Draw from your own experiences and observations.
2. Don't be afraid to tackle subjects that are important to you, even if they're challenging.

3. Experiment with different styles of humor to see what feels most natural.
4. Be willing to evolve your voice over time as you grow as a comedian and person.

Your stage persona is closely related to your comedic voice but focuses more on how you present yourself on stage. It's the character you embody when performing. This doesn't mean creating a fake personality, but rather an amplified version of yourself that translates well to the stage.

For instance, Sarah Silverman's stage persona is known for its combination of sweetness and shock value. She often delivers controversial material with a innocent, almost child-like demeanor, creating a comedic contrast. This persona is an extension of her real personality but heightened for comedic effect.

Remember, expressing your material effectively is as much about practice and experience as it is about natural talent. Record your performances, study how different techniques impact your comedy, and be willing to experiment and evolve your approach over time.

Exercises: Solo Brainstorming Sessions Using Specific Comedy-Generating Techniques; Pair Exercises for Crafting Jokes and Refining Punchlines

Solo Brainstorming Sessions Using Specific Comedy-Generating Techniques

The Observation Journal

Duration: 30 minutes daily for a week

Materials: Notebook or note-taking app

Exercise:

- Set aside 30 minutes each day to observe your surroundings and interactions.
- Write down at least 10 observations daily, focusing on quirks, inconsistencies, or absurdities you notice.
- At the end of the week, review your observations and highlight those with comedic potential.
- Choose the top 3 observations and spend 15 minutes on each, exploring different angles for jokes.

Example: Jerry Seinfeld famously used this technique, jotting down observations that later became iconic bits like his routine about airplane food.

The Reverse Angle Technique

Duration: 45 minutes

Materials: Paper and pen

Exercise:

- Write down 5 common beliefs or situations.
- For each, ask "What if the opposite were true?" and write down the reverse scenario.

- Spend 5 minutes exploring the comedic possibilities of each reversed scenario.
- Choose the most promising reverse angle and develop it into a full joke or bit.

Example: Instead of "the customer is always right," explore a world where "the customer is always wrong." How would businesses operate? What absurd policies might exist?

The "What If" Game

Duration: 30 minutes

Materials: Timer, paper, and pen

Exercise:

- Set a timer for 2 minutes.
- Write down as many "What if..." questions as you can think of, no matter how absurd.
- When the timer ends, review your questions and circle the 3 most promising ones.
- Spend 8 minutes on each circled question, exploring the comedic possibilities and potential joke structures.

Example: "What if plants screamed when you cut them?" How would this change gardening? Vegetarianism? Office decor?

Pair Exercises for Crafting Jokes and Refining Punchlines

The Setup Swap

Duration: 30 minutes

Exercise:

- Each comedian writes 5 joke setups without punchlines.
- Exchange setups with your partner.
- Spend 15 minutes crafting punchlines for your partner's setups.
- Share your punchlines and discuss which ones work best and why.
- Collaborate to refine the most promising jokes.

This exercise helps you practice creating punchlines for unfamiliar setups, enhancing your ability to find unexpected angles.

The Punchline Polisher

Duration: 40 minutes

Materials: Existing jokes that need refinement

Exercise:

- Each comedian presents 3 jokes they've been working on but feel need improvement.
- For each joke, follow this process:
  1. Comedian A performs the joke.
  2. Comedian B offers 3 alternative punchlines or tags.
  3. Both discuss the alternatives and choose the strongest option.
  4. Collaborate to further refine the chosen punchline.
- Switch roles and repeat for Comedian B's jokes.

This exercise helps you explore different angles for your punchlines and learn to collaborate on joke writing.

The Premise Expansion Challenge

Duration: 45 minutes

Exercise:

- Choose a simple premise or observation (e.g., "Online dating is weird").
- Set a timer for 5 minutes. Both comedians independently write as many jokes or angles on this premise as possible.
- Share your ideas and identify the 3 most promising ones.
- Spend 10 minutes collaboratively developing each of these 3 ideas into full jokes.
- Perform the resulting jokes for each other and provide feedback.

This exercise helps you generate multiple angles from a single premise and practice rapid joke development.

CHAPTER 9
STEPS AND PROCEDURES FOR EXCELLENT PERFORMANCE

For comedians, mastering performance skills is crucial for connecting with audiences and bringing their jokes to life. While having well-written material is important, the true challenge lies in performing live on stage. This chapter aims to guide aspiring comics in honing their comedic performance through focused practice.

Performing comedy is different from everyday conversation because it involves capturing attention, highlighting punchlines, and engaging the audience using timing, gestures, and vocal variety. Like any performing art, developing these skills requires consistent effort. By learning and regularly practicing techniques such as delivery practice, refining stage presence, and managing unexpected moments, emerging comedians can feel confident and professional in live performances.

Preparing Mentally and Physically for Performances

Performing comedy live demands thorough preparation both mentally and physically. This section delves into essential preparations to achieve an optimal performance state.

Emotional and physical readiness are key to cultivating confidence, enabling comedians to authentically express themselves on stage. Establishing pre-show rituals helps maintain focus and allows performers to relax fully into each performance. Aspiring comics who invest in thorough preparation benefit from heightened presence and stronger connections with their audience. This commitment to readiness enhances the overall comedic experience.

Mental Prep Techniques

Positive Mindset Exercises

Developing strong mental preparation techniques is essential for comedians to enhance their comedic resilience. Here are some daily activities that can uplift mood and bolster morale:

1. **Watch Inspirational Comedy Specials:** Enjoying favorite comedy shows that inspire laughter nourishes the spirit and boosts morale.
2. **Gratitude Journaling:** Writing down things you're grateful for can provide a centered perspective by focusing on life's blessings, including your own humor and talents.
3. **Affirmations:** Daily affirmations of your comedic abilities reinforce confidence while letting go of unrealistic expectations helps build a relaxed approach to performing.

Engaging in these positive mindset rituals, which foster laughter, gratitude, and self-acceptance, supports comedians in approaching each performance with creativity and ease.

Visualization Practices

Imagine and mentally rehearse every detail of your performance. Visualize delivering your jokes effortlessly, feeling the energy of an engaged audience, and experiencing the sensations of hitting each key point perfectly. Envision receiving appreciative applause and feeling a sense of satisfaction at the end of your show. Pre-experiencing these moments through visualization prepares you mentally and emotionally for the real performance, enhancing your readiness for catharsis on stage.

Affirmation Routines

Create positive self-talk routines that boost your confidence. Repeat affirmations about your comedic talents and the quality of your material regularly. Affirm your intention to share humor that brings joy freely to your audience. Thank yourself in advance for your dedication and perseverance, inspiring continued passion for your craft. These affirmation rituals help you embrace vulnerability as a natural part of personal and comedic growth, encouraging you to take bold risks and maintain a focus on the rewards essential for comedy success.

Physical Prep Drills

Preparing physically before a comedy performance is crucial for optimal delivery. Here are effective drills and routines to consider:

- **Warm-up Exercises:** Before going on stage, perform flexibility stretches to release any muscle tension that could hinder your movements. Vocal exercises such as elongating vowels or practicing tongue twisters help loosen inhibitions and prepare your voice for performance. Using drama techniques like "hot seating" can also help access authentic emotions, enhancing your connection with the audience.
- **Power-up Routines:** Boost your energy just before showtime with quick routines. Activities like a five-minute jump rope session or a light jog around the venue wake up your body physically. Using invigorating essential oils like mint or

eucalyptus can heighten your awareness. Listening to affirming, upbeat music playlists uplifts your mood, translating into inner confidence and outer joy.

- **Grounding Methods:** Stay calm and centered during the high-stakes moments of your performance with grounding techniques. Practice deep breathing to release worries and tensions with each exhale. Try progressive muscle relaxation exercises to systematically relax your muscles and calm your body. Visualize yourself grounded, like roots extending from your feet, drawing strength and stability from your supporters and surroundings.

Focus Rituals

Establish dedicated rituals to center your mind and ward off distractions before the show. Activities like journaling, meditation, or quiet prayer help settle your thoughts. Spending time alone in a green room with calming solo activities reduces mental chatter. Deep listening with binaural beats or soothing instrumental music can regulate breathing and energy levels, preparing you for performance mode.

Pre-Show Nutrition

Maintain steady energy and mental clarity on stage with strategic nutrition. Choose light, nutrient-dense foods such as fruits, vegetables, and complex carbs like oats or sweet potatoes to stabilize blood sugar levels. Herbal teas can calm nerves and hydrate for vocal clarity and lung capacity. Small protein snacks provide sustained energy without feeling sluggish before the show.

Energizing Motivational Tools

Use motivational tools to ignite passion and motivation before performing. Watch inspiring clips from comedy idols who have achieved success through dedication. Listen to uplifting music to boost your mood and energy levels. Writing heartfelt thank-you notes to supporters cultivates gratitude and transforms nerves into excitement. Keep an affirming journal to remind yourself of the joy in your craft and why you love what you do. Establishing custom pre-show rituals instills optimism and empowers emerging talent.

Rehearsing With Purpose

Practicing regularly is really important for comedians who want to get really good on stage. This section talks about different ways to practice that help you improve. Doing specific exercises helps you get better at delivering jokes and feel more confident. Recording yourself practicing lets you see what you can improve. Getting feedback from friends helps you see things from different perspectives. Using this feedback and practicing a lot helps you learn faster. Comedians who practice a lot and set clear goals get better quickly. Practicing with purpose helps you improve your skills faster, so you can entertain audiences and make them remember your performances.

Rehearse for Timing

Regularly practicing ensures that your timing is perfect, making each joke hit just right. Time your entire delivery to find the natural rhythms of each joke. Practice switching between speeds to find the perfect timing for each part. Master the art of strategic pauses to build anticipation effectively. Record your performances and see where longer pauses or breaks got the best reactions. Consistent practice will make these rhythms second nature and maximize the impact of your punchlines.

Rehearse for Emphasis

Focus on emphasizing key parts of your jokes naturally during your delivery. Mark the words you want to highlight and practice saying them in different ways to find the best interpretation. Experiment with different tones and pitches to see which ones make your emphasis most powerful or surprising. Record yourself emphasizing different words to discover new ways to add meaning. Feedback will help you find the most engaging ways to emphasize.

Rehearse Characters

Give each character a distinct voice and personality. Use physical gestures to develop unique traits for each character. Practice changing accents until each character sounds authentic without effort. Before recording, get into character to ensure consistency when reviewing. Ask friends for feedback to see if they can distinguish between characters based on their unique nuances. By dedicating time to your characters, you'll bring them to life with lasting personalities.

Rehearse Flow

Achieving smooth transitions between segments captivates audiences. Time your entire sets, running through your material without pauses. Practice seamlessly moving between acts using callbacks or taglines. Identify any stiffness in adding taglines to promote coherence. Record your runs to gauge where enjoyment peaks, indicating natural rhythms. With repetition, you'll develop instinctive continuity.

Rehearse Off Script

Prepare for unpredictable scenarios with improvisational rehearsals. Practice thinking quickly using prompts or playing "Yes, and..." games. Embrace unscripted questions, crafting witty responses. Review recorded impromptu sessions for ideas to enrich your existing material. Regularly improvising builds confidence for handling surprises during live shows.

Rehearse Delivery Dynamics

Keep your comedy routines entertaining with vocal agility through varied dynamics. Practice adjusting volume, speed, and inflections for different joke styles. Record softer deliveries to ensure nuances come across clearly. Experiment to find the highest energy level you can sustain without exhaustion. Seek feedback on where dynamic shifts effectively engage the audience. Mastering versatility keeps your audience captivated.

Rehearse Material Organization

Craft a well-sequenced routine to maximize enjoyment and audience recall from start to finish. Map out your entire set, arranging jokes in a logical or thematic order. Time transitions between different idea clusters to assess natural pacing. Rehearse your closers extensively to leave a lasting impression. Get feedback to confirm the overall impact of your programming. Strategic organization optimizes entertainment value.

Rehearse With Intent

Focus your rehearsals with specific, achievable goals using S.M.A.R.T. criteria and isolated filming. Set weekly practice targets, such as improving punchline clarity. Film isolated rehearsals to honestly assess specific skills. Repeat routines focusing solely on timing or characterizations. Solicit feedback that addresses your goals, like improving enunciation or timing, for precise refinement. Accountability in drilling improves your skills significantly.

Rehearse Adaptations

Build flexibility through diverse rehearsal scenarios to handle unpredictability. Practice adjusting the length of your acts to suit different environments sensitively. Embrace rehearsal surprises to develop composed mastery in handling uncertainty. Record sessions condensing anecdotes or transitioning material mid-routine to simulate real performance challenges, strengthening your confidence under pressure. Thorough preparation ensures you're ready for on-the-fly adaptations during live performances.

Developing Stage Presence

Having a great stage presence can really captivate the audience and make your performance shine. This section explores ways to build a likable and commanding persona on stage. Your presence comes from embracing your inner strengths and showing joy outwardly. Regular practice helps you become more confident as you grow. Aspiring comedians learn that being genuine, open, and positive is key to developing their presence. Mastery comes from hard work, but it starts with small steps along the way. With the right guidance, new talents can develop an irresistible magnetism on stage that really delights the crowd.

Presence Starts Within

Self-confidence starts with being kind to yourself. Reminding yourself of your good qualities helps convey humor with the intention of lifting spirits. Writing about what you're thankful for, even your mistakes, helps you see opportunities clearly. Imagining yourself spreading positivity turns nervousness into excited energy. Remembering what motivates you keeps you going, especially on tough nights. Working on yourself on the inside shows on the outside over time.

Connect With Authenticity

Sharing personal stories and lessons between jokes helps people connect with you on a deeper level. Being open about your own imperfections helps you connect with your audience. Responding naturally to what happens shows your quick wit and flexibility. Performing material that means something to you adds passion to your act. Audiences love seeing the real you.

Engage With Enthusiasm

Being genuinely joyful can really lift the mood in the room. Smiling and making eye contact spread cheer effectively. Using your body to tell stories makes them more exciting. Briefly interacting with the audience warmly keeps everyone engaged. When you're having fun, it inspires others to have fun too.

Command The Stage

Be confident and comfortable on stage. Practice breathing calmly to stay in control. Feeling stable and grounded lets you move freely. Adjust your volume and pace to fit the room. End your shows gracefully, welcoming applause confidently. Feeling at ease lets your wit shine brightly.

Use Facial Expressions

Your face can convey humor just as much as your words. Practice making subtle expressions that clarify jokes. Let genuine smiles and laughter come naturally. Connect with your audience through eye contact. Use expressions like raised eyebrows or head tilts to make your stories vivid. Expressive faces make even simple jokes come alive.

Employ Gestures

Use your body to bring jokes to life with carefully practiced movements. Match your physical gestures with your verbal timing. Act out jokes with mime or pantomime. Use full-body expressions to bring characters to life. Move around the stage to keep things interesting. Engaging storytelling brings your jokes to life visually.

Harness Wardrobe

Choose outfits that reflect your comedic style confidently. Try different styles to see what fits your material best. Use accessories sparingly to enhance your presentation without distracting from your act. Find clothes that fit well and flatter your best features. Wear versatile outfits that let you move comfortably. Your attire should complement your persona positively.

Showcase Passions

Share your genuine interests to connect with your audience. Use your knowledge of niche topics to add depth to your jokes. Share hobbies or talents that entertain while staying true to yourself. Use props creatively to add humor to your act. Adding layers of relatability makes your performance more memorable.

Exercises: Solo Visualization and Relaxation Exercises for Preparing for Performances; Pair Exercises for Practicing Stage Presence and Audience Interaction Techniques

Solo Visualization and Relaxation Exercises for Preparing for Performances

The Success Visualization

Duration: 15 minutes

Exercise:

- Find a quiet, comfortable space where you won't be disturbed.
- Close your eyes and take several deep breaths to relax.
- Imagine yourself arriving at the venue, feeling confident and prepared.
- Visualize the entire performance in detail:
  - See yourself walking on stage, the lights, the audience.
  - Hear the sound of your voice, clear and strong.
  - Feel the laughter and positive energy from the audience.
  - Imagine delivering your best jokes flawlessly.
  - Visualize the standing ovation at the end of your set.
- Hold this successful image in your mind for a few moments.
- Slowly open your eyes, carrying that feeling of success with you.

The Body Scan Relaxation

Duration: 10 minutes

Exercise:

- Lie down or sit comfortably with your eyes closed.
- Starting from your toes, focus on each part of your body in turn.
- For each body part:
  - Tense the muscles for 5 seconds.
  - Release the tension, focusing on the feeling of relaxation.

o   Take a deep breath before moving to the next body part.
- Work your way up through your legs, torso, arms, and face.
- Once you've relaxed your whole body, take three deep breaths.
- Open your eyes, feeling calm and centered.

The Positive Affirmation Ritual

Duration: 5 minutes

Exercise:

- Stand in front of a mirror.
- Take three deep breaths.
- Look yourself in the eye and repeat the following affirmations (or create your own):
    o   "I am funny and talented."
    o   "I connect easily with my audience."
    o   "My performance brings joy to others."
    o   "I am confident and in control on stage."
    o   "I handle unexpected situations with ease and humor."
- Repeat each affirmation three times, speaking clearly and confidently.
- Smile at yourself in the mirror before finishing.

Pair Exercises for Practicing Stage Presence and Audience Interaction Techniques

The Mirror Exercise

Duration: 20 minutes

Exercise:

- Stand facing your partner, about arm's length apart.
- One person is the "leader," the other the "mirror."
- The leader slowly moves, focusing on facial expressions and body language.
- The mirror copies these movements as exactly as possible.
- After 5 minutes, switch roles.
- Discuss how it felt to lead and follow, and what you noticed about each other's movements.

This exercise helps develop body awareness and control, crucial for stage presence.

The Heckler Response Drill

Duration: 30 minutes

Exercise:

- Take turns performing 2-minute segments of your material.
- The non-performing partner plays the role of a heckler, interrupting with comments or questions.
- The performer must respond to the heckle and smoothly return to their material.
- After each round, discuss effective responses and areas for improvement.
- Gradually increase the difficulty and frequency of the heckles.

This exercise helps improve quick thinking and audience management skills.

The Energy Matching Game

Duration: 25 minutes

Exercise:

- One partner begins telling a story, establishing a certain energy level (e.g., excited, calm, frustrated).
- The other partner must interrupt and continue the story, matching the energy exactly.
- Switch back and forth every 30 seconds, maintaining the energy level.
- After 5 minutes, change to a new energy level and repeat.
- Discuss the challenges of maintaining and matching different energy levels.

This exercise helps develop the ability to control and adapt your energy on stage.

The Crowd Work Simulation

Duration: 40 minutes

Exercise:

- Create character cards with different audience member types (e.g., shy person, loud laugh, easily offended).
- Take turns performing 5-minute sets, with the non-performing partner playing 2-3 different audience members.
- The performer must engage in crowd work, interacting with these "audience members."
- After each set, discuss effective techniques and areas for improvement.
- Switch roles and repeat.

This exercise helps improve audience interaction skills and adaptability.

BONUS

Recommended Reading List

For further education and inspiration as you continue honing your comedic craft, consider exploring some of these seminal texts that deepen understanding across various angles:

- **American On Purpose by Craig Ferguson** - A revealing autobiography from the former Late Late Show host and prolific stand-up sharing his colorful life story and passion for performance.
- **Bossypants by Tina Fey** - A brilliantly funny read covering the Emmy-winning comedian/producer's career journey, from early improv success to breaking barriers on Saturday Night Live and beyond.
- **Comedy Drama by Bob Odenkirk** - The acclaimed writer/producer shares experiences working with industry greats while highlighting important issues like cultivating creativity and embracing failure.
- **They Call Me Ralph:** An Autobiography by Richard Lewis - An hilarious and touching memoir from a modern comedy icon, offering behind-the-scenes insights into the constant self-doubt and dedication required for a career in stand-up.

Glossary Of Comedy Terms

Beat: A deliberate pause inserted into a joke or comedy act to enhance timing and impact.

Blue comedy: A form of humor that explores profane, shocking, or taboo topics, often involving crude language or sexual themes.

Brainstorming: A creative process where comedians generate numerous ideas or topics without restriction to develop new material.

Callback comedy: A technique where a joke reintroduces an element from a previous joke to add humor.

Callback: A comedic technique where a previous joke or idea is referenced to create laughter.

Character-based comedy: A comedic approach that involves portraying distinct, exaggerated characters or accents to amuse the audience. It requires strong skills in embodying different personas.

Character-based comedy: A style that features exaggerated and unrealistic characters through accents, voices, or quirks, rather than the comedian's real persona.

Clean comedy: Humor that avoids vulgar language or risqué subjects to appeal to a broader audience.

Clean comedy: Comedy that steers clear of profanity, explicit content, or offensive topics, making it suitable for family audiences.

Closer: The final joke or act in a comedian's set, designed to elicit a strong laugh and leave a memorable impression.

Crowd work: Unscripted interaction and banter with the audience, not part of the planned routine.

Delivery: The way a comedian uses vocal and physical techniques to enhance the humor in their jokes.

Heckler: An audience member who disrupts the show by trying to provoke or insult the comedian.

Heckler: A disruptive individual in the audience who attempts to provoke or interrupt the comedian, often by yelling insults.

Improvisational comedy: A type of live comedy that relies on spontaneous, unscripted interaction and audience participation. It can include long-form improv shows or short scenes and games.

Joke construction: The process of writing a joke, typically involving a setup and a punchline.

Observational comedy: Humor derived from everyday observations and minor details, often related to relationships, social situations, or common annoyances, making it widely relatable.

One-liner: A brief joke that delivers a punchline in as few words as possible, testing the comedian's timing and wordplay.

Premise: The central theme or topic around which a series of related jokes are constructed.

Punchline: The final part of a joke where the humorous element is revealed, intended to get the biggest laugh.

Punchline: The end of a joke that delivers the humor or surprise, aiming for the largest laugh.

Rehearsal: The practice process comedians use to refine their material and delivery before performances.

Riffing: Spontaneous comedic improvisation or expanding on a previous idea in a lively, back-and-forth manner, often used in joke development.

Routine: A sequence of jokes, stories, or sketches that make up a comedian's performance.

Setup: The initial part of a joke that provides context or background before the punchline.

Set-up: The part of a joke that introduces the context leading up to the punchline.

Storytelling comedy: A comedic style that involves telling long, humorous narratives about personal experiences, incorporating jokes and creating a connection with the audience.

Tag: A brief, additional humorous comment or callback added to the end of a joke.

Timing: The control of pacing, rhythm, and pauses in delivering a joke, crucial for maximizing laughter.

CONCLUSION

We've reached the end of our deep dive into the fascinating world of stand-up comedy. By exploring its rich history, psychology, diverse styles, and practicing key techniques, you're now equipped with a solid foundation to begin your own comedic journey. I hope this guide has not only deepened your appreciation for stand-up as an art form but also given you the confidence and skills to share your humor authentically.

While the road ahead as a comedian will have its challenges, remember the lessons you've learned here. From crafting routines to overcoming stage fright, you now have proven methods to develop strong sets, refine your unique voice, and continually grow creatively. Whether your goal is to headline big venues or entertain at local open mics, this framework provides a strong starting point.

Ultimately, comedy is about connecting with others through laughter, not just seeking fame or glory. Stay true to yourself, develop material that reflects your genuine perspective and passions, and treat everyone with empathy and respect. This approach will serve you well, whether you're performing in small venues or large arenas.

As you move forward, establish a disciplined writing routine, consume diverse comedy content, and perform regularly at local clubs to refine your act. Embrace constructive feedback and learn from every performance. Mastery comes with time and experience, so don't be discouraged by early challenges.

Continue to evolve your act, stay current with cultural trends, and explore new comedic styles. Above all, maintain the joy and spontaneity that make comedy so captivating. With persistence and dedication, you'll gain confidence, refine your timing, and command any audience effortlessly.

Utilize online platforms to build your brand and network within the comedy community. Showcase your talent professionally and consider filming sets to reach a wider audience. Collaboration and generosity will open doors in this close-knit industry.

Remember, comedy is a journey of growth and discovery. Keep pushing your boundaries, finding humor in life's ups and downs, and spreading joy wherever you go. Your adventure in comedy has just begun – embrace it with passion, perseverance, and a commitment to making people laugh. Best of luck on your comedic endeavors ahead!

Printed in Dunstable, United Kingdom

74374872R00130